THE EMERGENCE OF BLACKROCK

First edition. October 10, 2024.

Copyright © 2024 Edward Branson.

ISBN: 979-8227785473

Written by Edward Branson.

Table of Contents

The Emergence of BlackRock

Edward Branson

Prologue

What he reveals, what he builds with small impressionistic touches, is the rise to power of Larry Fink, the master of the new financial behemoth, BlackRock. When I close my eyes and think of Larry and BlackRock now, the image that comes to mind is that of a Godzilla emerging from the mega-crisis of 2008 and advancing towards us. What makes this book even more distinctive lies in its genesis. It should never have existed. This comical and frightening object that you hold in your hands was supposed to be a preface, but things went awry. I became a helpless witness to what I felt was an attempt at censorship.

It is delicate for me to use this word, but in the end, that is what it was. And that is what motivated the writing of this improbable object. I will not dwell here on the facts and their sequence—that is not really the role of a preface. The book tells it.

Larry and Robert were born from a dialogue and friendship between a free and committed publisher and his writer friend, a globetrotter of journalistic investigation and political combat (Denis Robert was the linchpin of the Clearstream scandal). The idea for the book came to us as an obvious necessity. I had to publish it; I had to be its publisher. But I also had to publish its direct counterpart, the very reason Denis turned his attention to BlackRock: the well-documented and authoritative book by the German journalist Heike Buchter: *BlackRock: These Financiers Who Seize Our Money.* The two books, though different, demonstrate in an implacable way the hidden workings and totalitarian objectives of BlackRock. Today, the multinational sees more than thirty trillion dollars pass through its Aladdin platform. Aladdin is Larry Fink's magic lamp—an indecipherable software, a terrifying informer, arbiter, and ultimately tyrant of global finance. BlackRock manages \$7.5 trillion in assets worldwide, including in France, where the firm owns around 4% of the CAC40, year in and year out—that is, the forty largest French companies listed on the stock exchange.

BlackRock is probably the greatest immediate and current threat, far more than Donald Trump's hairpiece or Xi Jinping's stern demeanor—and, in the short term, more so than the relentless march of climate change.

BlackRock is both the symbol and the reality of this monstrous marriage between totalitarian data technology and the omnipotence—half-gaseous, half-hallucinatory—of finance.

BlackRock is no longer just an economic or even political problem, which could be resolved with arguments and insights. BlackRock has become an uncontrollable madness, built on storytelling. BlackRock has become a myth.

Larry Fink, with his reassuring air of a fund manager and a brave American cowboy, has reinvented himself by becoming the man who whispers in the ear of the White House. He did it during the subprime storm. He continues today. He, too, has mutated into a legendary character.

A black legend. A legend that risks sweeping all of humanity into the impossible yet probable collapse of its immense house of cards, its Xanadu that will not kill its owner, but us. All of us—you, dear reader, whose money is managed by this good Larry, like everyone else. Yes, it is you who will be forced to whisper "Rosebud" before taking your last breath.

From its title, *Larry* accomplishes the vital gesture that is essential for our survival today: to restore a name, a humanity—at once banal and pitiful, and so necessary—to this inventor of the most dreadful software for spying, canning, and transforming human work into 0s and 1s, and therefore of man in general.

Page after page, this book resists and refuses; refuses the blind madness of the Aladdin software that crushes and manipulates economic data, holds its own against everyone—from politicians to big bosses—and reigns over the destiny of the economy. Page after page, this book gives back a man's name to the coming catastrophe. It wakes us up from the long nightmare where we see ourselves heading straight into the wall automatically—or rather, algorithmically.

Page after page, reader, this book invites you, in turn, to address Larry, and to say to him: "Larry, if you are a man, if you are, as you believe, a good American, a good nice guy, unplug your wonderful lamp, and return as quickly as possible your $7.5 trillion to those who truly own it. Not only to the retirees whose fortune you concentrate but to all of us. You have become, by a combination of schizophrenic circumstances, the guarantor and the guru of our future. All this power concentrated in your hands alone, Larry, you know it well, is the origin of the greatest delirious outburst that has ever afflicted the brain of the world economy."

In fact, reader, the only defense we have left is to remember that behind our assets, there is Larry and Robert. That is to say, all of us. And we must shout it as quickly as possible. At the end of the book, you will see a letter. This is a way for us to turn literature into a fight. Let Larry and BlackRock know what you think.

Chapter 01

———

Larry and I have a long history. Even though an ocean separates us, we were born on the same planet. Larry is six years older than me. His father was a shoe salesman in Los Angeles (western United States) and his mother was an English teacher. My mother was a seamstress, and my father was an engineer for EDF in Thionville (eastern France). Larry studied political science and earned a master's degree in business administration from the University of California in 1976, the same year I graduated. I studied psychology in Nancy until I obtained a DEA in psycholinguistics. In terms of the length of studies, you could say that I beat him by a short head.

I'm not showing off; I'm narrating.

In terms of assets, that's another matter. Apart from my house and an old Jaguar, I have no stocks, no savings plan, and no second home. Larry earned $25 million in income and BlackRock shares last year, making him the third highest earner on Wall Street. Two old bankers just beat him: the boss of Morgan Stanley (27 million) and the one who has held the top spot for years: Jamie Dimon, the boss of JPMorgan (31 million). This annual salary also places him behind Neymar, Messi, and Ronaldo, but slightly ahead of Mbappé. The story does not mention what other stock market or real estate income Larry has. He is very discreet about his investments. However, Bloomberg let slip in April 2018, announcing that Larry was entering the big family of billionaires, as the channel's journalist reported that he had just exceeded a billion in personal fortune, mainly thanks to the large number of BlackRock shares he owns. His score—while enviable—does not allow him to enter the top 100 richest men in the world. On the other hand, in the ranking of the most powerful, Forbes placed him in twenty-eighth position in 2018, behind Xi Jinping, Putin, and Trump, but far ahead of many other influential bosses and politicians. Since the ranking has existed, his rating has only climbed, and I bet you that he will enter the top 10 in 2020. Of course. Slowly, but as surely as BlackRock extends its influence on the globe. And, Forbes or not, he will obviously be number one in 2021. Larry Fink, Master of the Universe. That's a man. He will have his name gilded in fine gold on business cards that he will then hand out without smiling (Larry has a very limited sense of humor) during his travels in Europe or Asia. Larry likes wealth, not opulence. He is very secretive about what he earns and amasses. A farm in North Salem with cows and horses, a villa in Aspen in the Colorado resort for the happy few—Larry does not multiply, unlike many of his banker friends, flashy real estate investments. Our man especially likes power and reading fear or admiration in the eyes of his interlocutors. The question I ask myself when I see him on television or read the annual letter sent to the tens of thousands of entrepreneurs linked to BlackRock could be summed up as: "Does he know where he is going and what he is doing?" I fear the answer is negative.

Deep down, apart from his wife and three children, I think Larry doesn't give a damn about what happens to others. He's a libertarian, binary, and casual, who could take up Nekfeu's rap: "Your existence matters little to me if you're not my sidekick... People are nicer when you sign your contract... Dedication to you who said you didn't believe in me... Today I do live shows, I make money, I live my life... So I don't give a damn, I don't give a damn about anything..." A story told by a former BlackRock executive says a lot about Larry's deep nature. He flies over the Atlantic in his jet. Suddenly he gets the idea to make a stopover in Germany to see Angela Merkel. He asks his pilot to land in Frankfurt and calls his correspondent to arrange an interview with the German chancellor... five hours later. Sweat of the guy who, despite all his efforts, does not succeed in this feat and instead finds him a one-on-one with the vice president of BMW. The meeting begins, the two guys chat. Larry realizes that he is bored and that he does not care much about the underboss. He takes out his cell phone and types a text message to organize his next meeting, "leaving his interlocutor speechless," specifies a witness of the scene. Larry and I have never crossed paths. I have seen him on TV several times. I do not think that is the case for him. I mean, I do not think he has seen me on TV. Larry has a very regulated life. At least that is the image he wants to give. He gets up at 5 o'clock every morning and leaves his building on the Upper East Side of Manhattan three-quarters of an hour later to go in a limousine to his office at BlackRock. Larry reads three newspapers—always the same ones—every morning: The Wall Street Journal,

The Financial Times, and The New York Times, before starting his meetings and videoconferences.

The BlackRock building is an ordinary tower located on Park Avenue, with a shopping mall and a Starbucks on the ground floor. Nothing to do with the luxury displayed by Trump Tower or the Goldman Sachs palace on the Hudson. Lloyd Blankfein, the head of the investment bank, dropped two billion to show the world and his trading and banking buddies the insolent wealth of his shop. Larry is more modest and smarter. He wants to show that he is rich but thrifty. In terms of influence on the world's business, BlackRock and its executives have largely surpassed the suits and ties of Goldman. And for any journalist accustomed to the mysteries of Wall Street, Larry no longer plays in the same league as Lloyd. The most powerful is rarely the most show-off.

Larry comes home at 6:30 to find his wife Lorri, whom he met in high school when he was seventeen. Larry and Lorri: the couple smells like a cover portrait for Reader's Digest, the magazine that has been enchanting the heartland of America since 1923. "At 10:30 p.m., he turns out the light," Fortune magazine's star journalist, Carol Loomis, tells us in a hagiographic piece that BlackRock's press office palms off on all the journalists who contact the multinational. So Larry takes care of our savings, goes to bed early, and works all the time. The message is getting through. When Larry has a problem, he submits it to Aladdin, BlackRock's artificial intelligence, and sends his PR people or lawyers to sort it out. He could even afford a hitman. I'd do the same as him, but I can't afford it. Okay, I admit: my worries are not of the same ilk. He deals in geopolitics, high-frequency trading. I deal in political editorials, low-frequency hassles. A Lebanese trader based in London is filing multiple complaints against me under pretexts as diverse as defamation, insult, and invasion of his privacy. Even if he loses, he won't give up. I am everything he hates. He's ruining my life, but I let him do it. Since I'm negligent, an art gallery has been selling my paintings for two years without paying me. I always find an excuse to avoid confrontation. A litigious driver invented a violent reversing and a collision with his car by me to defraud my insurance. The accident never happened, but the guy has a witness. I work on myself so as not to get angry. Larry doesn't have these kinds of concerns. Since I resumed my daily work as editorial director of a television channel for leftists (second-level humor, I'm joking), meetings and conflicts have followed one another without me being able to control everything. The National Council of the New Resistance, which we are trying to launch, takes up a lot of my time. Emmanuel Macron and his new government, which looks very similar to the old one, even more so. Étienne Chouard's lovers harass me on the Internet and come to bother me at home. I left my books unfinished, my films in gestation, the script commissioned by a producer lying fallow. And then there's the house, the children, the family, basketball. My father, who lost his wife—my mother—can't get over it. Me neither, by the way, but that's another story. At the end of the lockdown, a friend sent me a letter asking me to take a break. According to her, I am engaged on too many fronts. "You should do some soul searching in the face of this overflow of activities. What void are you trying to fill?" she asks me. I don't need a psychoanalyst, more like a yogi master. Someone who can teach me how to make the right decisions. I'm going to reread Krishnamurti. Free myself from the known. But first, I have one last mission to accomplish. I called my friend back to thank her for her letter, and we talked:

"By defending lost causes, you've become a world champion of the type who gets himself into trouble all by himself," she tells me.

"I'm fine, I'm standing up and I'm in good shape."

"Guys always say that kind of thing before a stroke or a heart attack."

"Stop it, I'm telling you I'm fine... I'd rather be in my own skin than in Larry Fink's."

"Whose skin?"

"The boss of BlackRock."

"Is he a musician?" I explain to her who Larry is and my still vague project. At the time, I wasn't yet thinking of a book, more of a long article.

"As soon as a subject touches you, it's stronger than you," she mocks. "You go headlong."

I weakly deny it, but she insists:

"You have to reason coldly. You would gain by taking a step back…"

And she adds:

"Your problem is that you're not cunning enough, so you get yourself into trouble all by yourself."

I sigh and manage to change the subject. I may not be cunning, but I am tenacious. I believe in my lucky star. Should I confess to her that I am going to do the complete opposite of what she advises me to do?

The philosopher Bernard Stiegler has just committed suicide. I was reading his latest book *Qu'appelle-t-on panser?* to interview him at the start of the school year. He has been warning us for several years about the destructive madness of financial markets and algorithms. "When reason is lost," he writes, "all the technological powers that are in our hands as so many 'progresses of civilization' become weapons of destruction by which this 'civilization' becomes barbarism."

I read each sentence from Bernard Stiegler as an address to Larry Fink and what he is undertaking with BlackRock: creating a world above the world, playing the financial acrobat, juggling laws and customs to assert his dominant position on the financial markets, and accelerating the acquisition of shares and bonds in a lawless zone. BlackRock, his creation, through its hybrid and uncontrollable status as a global investment fund, innovates in what Stiegler calls the "technological Wild West." I was struck by this quote on the back of a previous book: "For the lords of economic war, in the disruption, which is a phenomenon of acceleration of innovation, it is about going faster than societies to impose models on them that destroy social structures and render public power powerless. It is, in a way, a strategy of paralyzing the adversary."

That's what happens with Larry. He paralyzes his opponents. He always shoots first.

And he's become too big to fail.

By transferring to society the risks it doesn't want to assume, while picking its clients' pockets, BlackRock can destroy the social structures of a country.

Too big to fail.

Never has the expression been more appropriate.

"Zero risk, man," Larry would say, squinting.

No one contradicts him, except for this little voice coming out of a very small book with a turbulent history:

"Stop your damn spiel, the systemic risk is total, man."

Chapter 02

There is a special vibration between Larry and me.

Even though I am aware that his concerns are a thousand miles from mine, we are made of the same flesh. We have problems of ego, love, and friendship. When our loved ones disappear, we suffer. We are mortal, aware of our finitude, and we wonder about the future of humanity. At least, I hope so. A writer is never retired, nor is an investment banker. While most of our contemporaries dream of a golden annuity and a peaceful end to life, Larry works tirelessly to capture the money of retirees, especially French ones. And at my level, I try, perhaps foolishly, to thwart his plans.

I forget a detail.

Larry collects, in his farm-museum in North Salem, about a hundred kilometers from New York, old battered gourds, weather vanes, yellowed photos, and cowboy saddles—everything he calls American folk art. A guy who collects weather vanes can't be fundamentally bad.

He may have been born under the Californian sun, but he reminds me of a Midwest redneck. A farmer from Iowa or Missouri, always on the cows' backsides, watching you from afar, squinting. Larry is a great manipulator, but he works in a binary way. In life, my friend, there is what is profitable and what is not profitable.

Manipulator + binary = formidable efficiency.

With his management degree in hand, Laurence Douglas Fink traveled the country and quickly became the head of the real estate credit department at First Boston in New York. Very quickly, he hit it big selling securitized mortgages. The success of these financial products, which were innovative at the time, was based on cascading resales of real estate loans. Twenty years later, they would cause the subprime crisis. Thanks to them, Larry went on to shine and climb the bank hierarchy, without suspecting the catastrophe to come.

Let's dwell on the subject for a moment. These innovative products were based on a compilation of more or less solid mortgage loans. Let's imagine that you invested in real estate by taking out loans secured by the buildings you bought. You invested in different cities, from New York to Detroit, via Sun City, a self-managed and bunkered city in Arizona for seniors.

In Sun City, with thirty-eight thousand inhabitants, the model is declining. The old people have ended up getting bored. Almost all of them are sellers and can't find anyone to buy their properties. In Detroit, they no longer build cars, they no longer do business, and real estate is collapsing. Fortunately, in New York, people still buy luxury penthouses. Let's say I have an apartment near Trump Tower. I'm going to securitize, consolidate all my real estate assets—my unsellable house in Sun City, my crappy building in Detroit, and my New York penthouse—into a single entity. Then I sell shares in what becomes a fund. A shady scheme. A dud. My real estate has become liquid, and I can get rid of it.

The houses in Detroit are falling apart. Old people are dying without having paid off their dream villas. Sun City is becoming Death Valley. Yet mortgage securities continue to sell like hotcakes. The return to reality will be cruel. Mortgage debt is increasing, but it remains hidden by many investors. In 2006, the first person to have seen and understood the scale of the disaster to come was a small financial analyst, Michael Burry. Thanks to his accurate predictions—and despite the denigration of Wall Street financiers—we find him again today because, fourteen years after having warned of the subprime crisis, he warns us against the financial cataclysm that could be caused by the gigantism and risky strategies of Larry Fink with BlackRock.

In 1987, a harbinger of the 2008 crisis, Larry had an indigestion of crap. The loss in value of real estate assets was much greater than what specialists call the "haircut," the minimum contribution for a purchase on credit. In France, the "haircut" is generally at least 30%. Thus, the banker who has a mortgage and has the right to sell 100% of the property can repay himself, even if the market falls by 30%. In the USA, this safety net is much less significant, and if there are only sellers, the bankers can lose their shirts. This is a bit like what happened to Larry. An aggravating circumstance for him: the American central bank, the Fed, seeing these difficulties in mortgage repayments looming, suddenly lowered its interest rates to avoid a crash, causing the massive resale of credits. Larry did not see it coming. He made First Boston lose $100 million in a single day—a bitter and memorable failure. He would experience the joys of the closet before leaving his job as a trader and building what would become BlackRock.

No matter its size, the probability that an asset will rise or fall is always one in two. When an extraordinary phenomenon disrupts the balance and certainties of financiers, like a butterfly that beats its wings without warning and causes a chain reaction, these financiers—generally arrogant and self-confident traders—are caught off guard. They had to put words to mask their ignorance, so as not to lose too much face. Traders named this unexpected chain of events "leptokurtic." A barbaric name used by Larry and the BlackRockers to fool us with learned words and not explain why their strategy screwed up and why you lost all your savings.

This failure that occurred early—he was thirty-three—formed a conviction in him: to succeed in finance, it is necessary to foresee the future and therefore to limit leptokurtic risks. Hence his obsession with predictive calculation and the assurance that ended up emerging from his persona.

"Larry Fink is the guy who makes you believe that any living phenomenon can be put into an equation," a wealth manager interviewed as part of this research told me.

If we think about this journey, BlackRock initially operated like a large provincial bank in the Midwest: Let's limit the risks, and avoid crazy things. Larry is very gifted, very cautious, but he could not have foreseen the gigantic success of his intuition. Initially, in his farmer's head, BlackRock was probably a kind of large shopping center for bankers—a hub, of which he would be the boss. Not this crazy machine, condemned to grow and expand to survive. Who could have imagined such a thing and such a destiny?

Technical sophistication, the creation of a unique artificial intelligence, was not supposed to work so well. When you read the first advertisements for financial products carried by BlackRock, you think that its displayed assurance, about returns on investment based on diabolical algorithms, seemed like hot air. Pure cowboy spiel with narrowed eyes.

Twenty years later, we are in a scenario like *Black Mirror*, the Channel 4 anticipation series taken over by Netflix. Larry has created a monster that is beyond him. BlackRock will soon touch even tiny margins on practically all stock market transactions on the planet. And, thanks to Aladdin, Larry is informed in real time about the financial state of all his clients and users.

He has access to the matrix of capitalism. He can read all the balance sheets of practically all the companies in the world. He knows what is at stake between competitors. He can thus privilege one or the other in the greatest secrecy.

He is the living god of capitalism.

Just that? No, even worse.

Chapter 03

———

It all started with a call from Florent Massot. It was 10 p.m., and I was at my father's for our first post-lockdown meeting. Usually, Florent calls me at more reasonable hours. His voice was tired. He didn't dare tell me the reason for his call right away, asked how I was, but I sensed that something was wrong.

It was about the preface I had given him a week earlier. I had sweated over reading, understanding, and writing a few intelligible pages about a big book on BlackRock that had come out four years earlier—the only book published in the world on the New York firm and its founder. I have a special history with this firm, named after a heavy metal band, and its boss, Larry Fink. I have been following them for over ten years, as well as Vanguard, State Street, the Koch brothers, Merrill, Goldman, and Lloyd Blankfein—in short, all the American champions of finance. I had called Florent a few months earlier, after watching a film on Arte, to alert him to the subject, with the opportunity to publish a book in French. We were in the midst of a debate on the pension reform proposed by Emmanuel Macron, and Larry Fink, the world champion in all categories of funded pensions, was eyeing the potential investments of French retirees. I had finally written a preface that held up, happy and relieved with my twenty-one pages, because the book was just waiting for it to go to print. Based on the journalist's explanations, the ending mentioned the increase in poverty as the only way out of Larry's strategy: "Larry wants to palm off his pension insurance on us, forgetting that Americans, while extending working hours, have lost 30% of their pensions since the 2008 crisis and the increased control of investment companies like BlackRock. The fact that Fink invites us to consider this risk in a relaxed manner is cynical. The attack on pension systems is Larry Fink's Great Work. BlackRock is the armed wing that aims to destroy the welfare state everywhere. [...] Larry Fink has mastered the art of ignoring the poor. And making them even poorer."

The book tells the story of the rise of the investment fund that now owns shares in tens of thousands of companies all over the world, and in France, where BlackRock owns 5% of about twenty CAC 40 companies and where Larry has his napkin ring at the Élysée. Heike Buchter, the German journalist, correspondent for *Die Zeit*, and author of the book published only in Germany, is not a writer or novelist. She tries to be educational in her book, but often, her long chapters on the practice of hedge funds and on ETFs—Exchange-Traded Funds—literally "funds traded on the stock exchange," are complicated to digest. That's what I tried to do in my preface, making fun of Larry a little. It was fair game.

Explaining finance is a tedious exercise, which first requires understanding it. Heike Buchter's book had the great merit of giving us a glimpse of the internal mechanics of BlackRock and of painting—in the background—the portrait of its mysterious boss. Like any mortal human being aged sixty-eight who sees the years go by, Larry Fink may no longer be as powerful in ten years. One day, another will take his place, but he is not the type to pass on the crown or let go of the banister. He will certainly keep an eye and a hand on BlackRock.

So, I wrote this damn preface. I'm happy with it. I sent it to Florent. He was delighted. He sent it to his publishing manager, who was delighted. She sent it to the lawyer, who was not delighted (lawyers who work for publishing houses often get angry because I give them a lot of work). The lawyer assured us that my preface was not defamatory. Without pushing myself too much, I have some experience in defamation matters, and I'm careful when I write to never cross the yellow line of insult or defamation. It doesn't make us immune to complaints, but it gives us a good chance of not losing too much money in the event of a lawsuit. Everything was going well until Florent's phone call...

"Something crazy is happening," he tells me.

I thought to myself that maybe he got an exclusive with the Dalai Lama and wanted me to accompany him to film a retreat in Tibet? Or that Emmanuel Macron had just called him to propose his lustful confession and he wanted me to ghostwrite?

But that wasn't what was worrying Florent, I guessed:

"Larry Fink wants to see us because he doesn't appreciate me making fun of him in my preface?"

"That's almost it," Florent replies. "BlackRock is more powerful than you thought. They don't want your preface..."

"You're kidding..."

"No, the Germans are stuck on what you wrote... The German publisher of *BlackRock: A Secret Power is Seizing Your Money*, alerted by the author Heike Buchter, refused to let my text, which they had been warned about for a long time, appear at the beginning of the book. My preface didn't break any rules, yet it didn't suit them."

"They say you're going too far. Heike is uncomfortable with your vision of BlackRock. Basically, what you wrote doesn't please her and scares her a little..."

There was a pause. I spontaneously told Florent that it wasn't that serious.

"It's not the end of the world. I lost a week. And I read a good book. Well, to be completely honest, the book was still a bit boring..."

"They also contacted BlackRock, and the lawyers got involved," Florent added. "The agent says it will be sorted out. I hope so, but I'm not sure. It's a bit strange, this turnaround."

Florent and I immediately, without consulting each other, thought the same thing. It wasn't me or my words that Heike was afraid of, but BlackRock. The story was becoming interesting. It was a striking demonstration of the power of this omnipresent firm in the financial world. And a sign that we had hit the nail on the head. If the reissue of Heike Buchter's book and its tiny preface (twenty-one pages all the same, running gag!) had gone down like a letter through the post, it would have been almost disappointing. Florent wanted to understand why the Germans had changed course so suddenly. Were the journalist and her editor under pressure? Was it last-minute stress and self-censorship? That evening, we didn't know. Florent was dejected. I was less so, and my father was getting impatient.

"We'll see tomorrow, Florent..."

Chapter 04

————

We had just finished the foie gras, and he had cooked two steaks with Cassegrain peas that were getting all dry. A thought from Machiavelli was running through my head:

"To govern is to put your subjects in a position to harm you and even to think about it."

BlackRock, so huge, so monstrous, so loaded with lawyers, communicators, and jurists, had created a psychological tension among journalists that probably prevented them from even considering harming it. Like, "Attacking Larry Fink? Don't even think about it."

This is precisely what a friend, worried about me writing on the subject, would tell me a few weeks later.

Behind my father, a Samsung television—flat screen, state-of-the-art—listed the known deaths from Covid: the singer Christophe, the politician Patrick Devedjian, the former president of OM, Pape Diouf. My father would lament, "They're all good guys... Maybe even Raymond Poulidor died from this crap," he would plead, without me trying to contradict him.

Since my mother passed, I try to have lunch or dinner with him regularly. We can't change the world. I listen to him tell me about his world, which is often limited to the deaths cluttering up his memories, his loneliness, and what the television tells him. And it tells him a lot. My father is a perfect target for his insurer, his banker, his mutual insurance company, his telephone operator. Television is an integral part of his life. It's a Samsung with a 135-centimeter diagonal. He subscribes to Canal Sat for 79.90 euros per month and has a slew of channels at his disposal.

My father, like many octogenarians, was sold the all-inclusive subscription and doesn't know how to get rid of it. Bolloré buys yachts thanks to these subscriptions. My father can watch Algerian cooking channels, windsurfing, yoga, Canal Frisson, Canal Polar, Canal Adult Only, golf channels, kung fu, meditation, learning Persian and Mandarin—all while his television universe is mainly focused on the news that he watches on repeat on LCI, BFM, CNews, the evening news on France 2 or TF1, and the news on France Lorraine. My father's life is punctuated by news feeds.

I had to explain to him how to watch football matches on BeIN Sport, which we sometimes watch while eating foie gras and Gruyère cheese. We swig our last bottles of Pomerol. Generally, after the first, when he wants to open the second, I tell him no, because I have a long way to go. And then, at half-time, I change my mind. We have our habits. My father must spend about eight hours a day, from fall to early spring, in front of his television. He has a special relationship with it. In spring and summer, he cuts his consumption by half and spends time in his garden.

My father is a good case study for BlackRock's influence on human brains and behaviors. Despite his eighty-five years, he has a sharp mind and is interested in politics, and a little in the stock market. He receives a good pension that largely covers his needs and has life insurance, which he fears—due to the crisis—will end up siphoned off by bankrupt banks. Even if it no longer concerns him, he worries about the return of the funded pension that Emmanuel Macron, Édouard Philippe, the liberal right, the "En Marche" movement, and Larry Fink are trying to pass, despite the virus.

"The population is aging; it is normal that young people work more than us. Ultimately, we were a generation of privileged people," confesses my father, repeating what the columnists of BFM, LCI, or CNews explained to him in endless debates.

Columnists = big fuckers.

I know, it's borderline, easy, and vulgar, but it's late.

And it's my book; I do what I want.

Chapter 05

On the way back, after paying three euros in tolls at Vinci and filling up with petrol under the starry sky, I tried to find a place near Metz—a small speck on the map—where BlackRock and Larry Fink had no control. But the now-tentacled hydra that is BlackRock owned more than 5% of Vinci (the tolls), Engie (energy), and Samsung (TVs). It had stakes in Ariane (rockets) and Eutelstat (satellites) and was collaborating with NASA and Google researchers on robots capable of space travel. BlackRock had also invested in dairy products (including the cheese we had eaten), cattle breeding, Cassegrain peas and carrots (through its shares in Bonduelle, the parent company), and wine—particularly the grands crus, which it encourages its clients to invest in. In January 2018, BlackRock even co-published a study aimed at taking stakes (via their famous ETFs) in the great wines of Burgundy and Bordeaux.

I continued my thoughts. BlackRock holds nearly 5% of Vivendi, the parent company of Canal and CNews, and Bouygues, the parent company of TF1 and LCI. A Kuwaiti fund, which invested in BeIN, is also a shareholder of BlackRock. Even the car I was driving that evening—my old Jaguar—was partly owned by BlackRock through its more than 5% stake in Tata Motors. Whether I had been driving a Peugeot, a Renault, or a Volkswagen, it would have been the same. The petrol in my tank? BlackRock owns more than 5% of Total.

Since Emmanuel Macron's election, Larry Fink has visited the Élysée Palace several times. The last visit was in January 2020 for the "Choose France" initiative: after Brexit, Macron and his team—led by him personally—redoubled their efforts to attract foreign investors. The BlackRock report on retirement savings has significantly influenced Macron's administration and Bruno Le Maire, with whom Larry had dinner in New York in June 2017, shortly after the Brexit announcement. By asking, "Why is BlackRock so powerful in Macron's France?" the newspaper *Marianne* was one of the first to address the thorny issue—largely ignored by other media—of Larry Fink's and BlackRock's influence at the Élysée. Nicolas Sarkozy might have given flashy $100,000 conferences for Lloyd Blankfein and Goldman Sachs in London and New York, but Larry Fink is more discreet in his methods of thanking or approaching politicians. Emmanuel Macron and François Hollande, the man who once declared finance his enemy, are easy prey for BlackRock. Larry hired Jean-François Cirelli to represent him in Paris. Cirelli, the former head of Gaz de France, had just sold off a jewel of the public service (gas, the heat of the poor) to Suez and Albert Frère under Sarkozy's government. He was the ideal candidate for this job as facilitator and strong-arm for BlackRock in France. Mathias Thépot, the journalist from *Marianne*, interviewed Michel Sapin, former Minister of Finance, who shared his experience of meeting Larry, a living legend he encountered during the "competitiveness council" meetings at the European Commission in Brussels: "Larry Fink is one of those who shape the opinion of this rather Manichean little world of economic decision-makers. He is an impressive personality," Sapin says, with a hint of admiration. "Above all, his speech on the economic attractiveness of a country carries weight," recalls this close friend of the former head of state, François Hollande.

Marianne reports that François Hollande's government "bent over backwards" to attract the attention of BlackRock, whose boss expected a president to make "reforms favorable to businesses." "And on this point, we can say that Emmanuel Macron, for whom France's attractiveness to the world of finance is a political marker, has not skimped on the means. In addition to lowering capital taxes and launching reforms of the labor market, unemployment insurance, health, and pensions, he maintains regular contact with Larry Fink," *Marianne* continues. The big boss was thus received several times at the Élysée and Matignon as soon as Macron was elected in late May 2017, before the representatives of the French association of asset managers were even invited. Welcome, Larry. The new president "is doing everything he can to show the Wall Street giant that France," *Marianne* explains, "is no longer the country known for resisting liberal economic reforms." Emmanuel Macron's efforts quickly pay off. Larry Fink calls on international investors to support France. Thanks to these close ties between Emmanuel Macron and Larry Fink, the French debt held by BlackRock doubled in one year, reaching 32 billion dollars. Larry also bought shares worth nearly 100 billion in CAC 40 companies. Everything is connected. They are all connected.

BlackRock is everywhere. In twenty years, no multinational in the world has expanded as rapidly. And no company has had such a hold on our lives.

Books are sometimes born from anger, from incomprehension, from a danger that looms on the horizon, or from a feeling and information that one wishes to share.

At the end of 2019, BlackRock directly managed a portfolio of $7,429 billion in financial assets. In addition, $21,000 billion was indirectly administered by BlackRock through its Aladdin software, used by the world's largest asset managers, including Vanguard, the sector's number two and major "rival" (and shareholder) of BlackRock.

BlackRock's turnover was then $14.5 billion, and its profits were $4.5 billion. This ratio between turnover and profit was twice the industry standard, making BlackRock a cash machine in a field that had not been one for a long time.

BlackRock is an anomaly.

Even though BlackRock does not have bank status (and does everything to avoid it in order to escape banking regulation), Larry Fink's megafund has become the "fake bank" of the financial markets. The difference is that BlackRock does not risk its shareholders' money—only that of its clients. A giant sleight of hand.

Heads, BlackRock wins. Tails, its clients lose.

Heads, I win; tails, you lose: it's a trickster's joke.

The trickster must persuade, convince, and lead. To find a good definition of a trickster, one should look to the best of them, the magician Jean-Eugène Robert-Houdin, who said: "A trickster is a fable designed to make each trick seem like the truth..." Without going that far, Wikipedia offers an interesting definition that immediately brings Larry and BlackRock to mind: "A 'swindler' is a person who uses speech to affirm qualities that seduce, emphasizing certain qualities to deceive the public, generally to sell products or services, things or ideas. He gives illusions an authentic character and circumvents the possibilities of clarification by using trickery."

The firm set up by Larry Fink is similar to a super operator—the operator of operators. The provider of values in a giant Monopoly where, whatever happens, everyone pays the bill...

Except that, in principle, the Monopoly bank is neutral with respect to the players. Since its creation, BlackRock has relied on the votes of the majority shareholders and the chairmen of the boards of directors of the companies in which it invests. This is no longer the case. The firm, as we will see, pays itself from all sides and changes the rules of the game according to its interests, which are not necessarily those of its clients. And these interests are sometimes even contradictory. With so many clients and interests, one ends up lost—perhaps intentionally, like in a Robert Houdin trick.

BlackRock's size and dominant positions exceed those of other players in the financial markets, leading to a tacit ultimatum: either you are with BlackRock, or you are against it. You are with it because you are led to believe that you will win and make money by letting them take the reins. That's also why you support the firm—the hope of quietly making money while paying minimal fees. And indeed, you often win, but at the end of the game, it's highly likely that you will lose.

I admit this is (a little) abrupt, but I will refine this assertion. It is one of my objectives.

Fasten your seat belts...

Chapter 06

In the days that followed, Florent insisted with the publisher and the author of the book to tell us what was wrong with the preface. He suggested, with my agreement, that I modify it, but he received no explanation. The agent, who had acted as an intermediary for the purchase of the rights to the German book, eventually sent him a response from the German publisher, Campus, which suggested that my text be used as a "separate" commentary. Although he considered my remarks "very good," the publisher thought that it would not be beneficial for Heike Buchter or for me to appear in the same work because our approaches would be different. The publisher added that a quote to be put on the cover of the book would be sufficient. He also suggested that I rewrite a new, very short preface of one to two pages, explaining why Heike Buchter's book is interesting for French readers. He insisted that everything must first be reread and validated by Heike Buchter.

While my preface was reread and validated by Florent's lawyer, the publisher fears our vulnerability in the face of BlackRock's power, likely revealing the real reason for the German retreat: the fear of legal action against the book due to – among other things – the preface. Heike Buchter herself drives the point home: "BlackRock has waited years for us to present it with such an open flank. They will crush us so quickly that we will have no chance of getting out of it," she writes.

They will crush us so quickly that we will have no chance of getting out of it...

We are clearly in the realm of fear, of threat. And of freedom of expression.

Isn't it our duty and the raison d'être of our professions to resist what threatens to crush us?

Florent had suggested that one of my paintings appear on the cover of the book or as an illustration inside. In these old works that have already been exhibited and have never caused any problems, I weave links between banks, multinationals, and investment funds. Here, the publisher and the author raise their voices and reach Godwin's point with astonishing speed. They veto it, indicating that my paintings could suggest (my) adherence to "conspiracy" theories. They fear that they will be accused, if one of my paintings appears on the cover, of "anti-Semitic innuendos." Heike takes up the pen and loads the boat a little more. She rejects this idea of illustration "vehemently not only for legal reasons but also for very personal reasons." She therefore does not want the link to the website (of the gallery exhibiting the paintings) to appear in the book either. Florent replied the next day, without us talking about it, that in the event of a trial in France, the publisher was on the front line and that Heike Buchter had nothing to fear, as he would cover all the legal costs. He suggested adding a note specifying that the preface only commits its author and himself. "A preface should make you want to read the book but is not necessarily a foil for the author. I have a thousand examples of prefaces that are not 100% based on the author's thesis and open onto something else or stand out if that is really the heart of the problem," he wrote. Florent kept me away from these letters. He was probably right. The exchanges continued throughout the month of May. The agent took over from the German publisher and Heike Buchter, who, visibly annoyed, refused all contact. Beyond the preface, while the manuscript updated with new information has been validated, the journalist and her editor want to reread the French translation and ask for a new deadline.

It is tense, because each remains stuck in their positions. At the end of May, a new message arrives, signed by the agent who asks to abandon the idea of including a preface, "even reworked," in the book. Neither the German author nor the editor thinks that, even if I make efforts to rewrite it, we will manage to create a preface with which they will feel "comfortable." Our approaches would be too far apart. Nevertheless, they are annoyed because they would still like me to participate in the launch of their book. They suggest that my preface be used as a promotional article in the media and assure that they regret this situation.

"So sorry!" concludes the missive.

And so are we.

The agent makes Florent understand that Heike has a family and a job as a financial journalist, that she lives in New York, and that she is not ready to lose status and notoriety for a preface. The argument holds up. We are at the heart of a central problem in our profession. More and more central, given the state of the forces present. I am well placed, given my ten-year history of fighting against Clearstream, to know that even if we win, legal proceedings launched with unlimited budgets only aim to exhaust the journalist and their editor—morally and financially. I will never blame a journalist or an editor who gives up and makes a choice opposite to mine.

I have explained myself enough about this. Clearstream lawyers and communicators have regularly mentioned, in the courts or in the media, my madness, my desire to destroy capitalism (sic), my obsession with fighting them, my hatred of Luxembourg. Nothing could be further from the truth. I am not an activist for anything other than writing, ethics, and... the truth. Mine, in any case. I find with BlackRock similar feelings to those I had with Clearstream. The scandal is not the same. It was paradoxically easier to demonstrate, on the basis of documents and testimonies, the double-dealing and hidden accounts and the dangerousness of the Luxembourg clearinghouse.

Ten years have passed. The financial world has become more complex. Trading robots have become widespread. The speed of transactions has accelerated. Their amounts have swelled. Artificial intelligence has improved. Their amounts have exploded. It all comes down to high-frequency trading and algorithms.

Systemic banks have grown even bigger but remain fragile and interconnected. Paradoxically, the value of banks, that is to say their market capitalization, has collapsed. Although BlackRock owns 6.5% of Société Générale, the latter is no longer worth much. It has lost 65% of its value in ten years. It is only worth 10 billion euros, and no one is launching a takeover bid for it anymore. It is almost a humiliation. The central banks are seeing their influence grow. The printing press is working. The speculative bubble is swelling. In this ambient and deregulated quagmire, BlackRock is playing Larry Fink's part. The firm's investments are gaining ground everywhere. Larry wants to make it indispensable, legal, and unattainable. The investment fund BlackRock has this in common with the clearinghouse Clearstream – besides the fact that both handle and store trillions of euros in their accounts – that they are freewheeling. Their gigantism, their technicality, have made them materially uncontrollable. The organ and its automatisms have taken precedence over human capacity to integrate all the data.

"It is not the technology that is toxic in itself, it is our inability to socialize it correctly," warns Bernard Stiegler. This is exactly the paradigm we are talking about.

As I reread myself, I try to imagine the details or turns of phrase that could have frightened a journalist anxious to preserve her sources in the financial sphere. When writing my preface, it seemed to me that I was only repeating Heike's enormous and indispensable work by connecting it to my own feelings and knowledge of these circles.

I did not see the problem. I still do not see it.

I had read a lot, well before Heike Buchter's book, on Larry Fink and international finance. He and a few others were subjects of investigations and obsessive questioning at one point in my life, around 2008, when Clearstream had campaigned against my investigations. I saw the name of BlackStone, from which BlackRock came, and that of Larry Fink regularly appear in the financial schemes of this parallel finance. With purchases of shares and bonds, they were nibbling away at European capitalism. The bankers were complicit. The judges were powerless. The politicians turned a blind eye.

We could have left it there. I took up my preface again, and I made confetti out of it. Florent published Heike's book for which he had already invested in translation, purchase of rights, and various charges—almost 20,000 euros. We forgot the fact that I was at the origin of this editorial project, advising Florent to take the rights to the book published by Campus, after watching the Arte documentary on BlackRock.

On its website, Campus, a publishing house founded in 1975, presents itself as having its headquarters in Frankfurt and New York and as an "independent and successful" publisher. Their program covers a "broad range" of subjects with an emphasis on economics, politics, society, history, careers, business, and social sciences. In addition to a wide range of German authors, Campus publishes Judith Butler, Jeremy Rifkin, and Paul Krugman... "The goal of Campus and its employees is to advance society and the individual," boasts the brochure. Campus books contribute to political, economic, and historical debates, and present the latest research results." Campus also deals in "personal development and careers in finance and business." When you look more closely at the catalog, you find a lot of investment advice books, like *The Ingeniously Simple Wealth Strategy, How to Get Rich in Norway, Manage Your Money like a Fucking Grown-Up...* And, more interestingly, books that Larry Fink could sponsor: *Invest with Confidence after Retirement* or *Invest with Confidence in Difficult Times, Exploit Your Opportunities for Wealth in Difficult Times, Financial Strategies for Late Beginners, Nothing Without Risk.* They teach you how to invest in risky, difficult times.

And no advice on how to give the fish to a German publisher whose house motto is also that of BlackRock. Just imagine them not afraid of possible conflict with the famous American investment firm, if we are to believe the author and the publisher. Campus is a subsidiary of the large Beltz group (300 employees, 120 titles per year), a German-language reference in psychology, education, and childhood, created in 1841. The financial publisher is only one branch of the group. The independent publisher is therefore a cog in a large German group that had done everything to crush our little book, translated by an equally small publisher.

Chapter 07

At the end of 2011, after the Court of Cassation ruled in my favor in my lawsuits against Clearstream, stating that my investigation was "serious, in good faith and served the general interest," the case was sent back to the Lyon Court of Appeal to assess the amount of damages. After ten years of battling the financial sharks, defending myself against accusations, and having my life disrupted, how much was that worth? A million euros? Two? Three? Ten? Forty-five, like the amount of moral damages awarded to Bernard Tapie three years earlier? By the end of the year, the Lyon Court of Appeal ruled and did not recognize my moral damages. I was only awarded reimbursement of my legal costs. In other words, a pittance, considering the turmoil this case had caused in my life and that of my loved ones over the past decade. The Lyon Court of Appeal considered the attacks I endured to be, in some way, part of the risks of being a journalist.

In the United States, I would have received a substantial settlement, but the Lyon magistrates, conservative and reluctant to acknowledge the grip of finance and multinationals like Clearstream on our economies and lives, did not want to set a precedent that would benefit other journalists and future whistleblowers. I should have counterattacked and appealed again to the Court of Cassation, but I was exhausted. I wanted to forget Clearstream and its complications. I wasn't depressed, but I could no longer do what I had been dedicated to for so many years: write. One of my books had been banned from sale and withdrawn from bookstores on the day of its release. It was the final straw. Despite my resilience, I was deeply affected. For months, I sat at my computer, unable to write a single coherent line. I was burdened with negative thoughts and troubling questions: why had books ceased to be the exclusive domain of our democracies?

To escape the mental trap and forget the trials, I sought refuge in an art gallery in Paris – Galerie W, run by a couple, Isabelle Euverte and Éric Landau. They probably saw an interest in my story. With Philippe Pasquet, a painter friend and drawing teacher, I found a new meaning in the words that haunted me. I began writing on canvases, inventing shapes. I no longer had the strength or desire to investigate but retained the anger to denounce the threat I sensed: the rise of BlackRock and the destructive influence of such investment giants on our economic and social fabric.

How did we reach the point where American pension funds decide the fate of our industries, trades, vineyards, and political life?

It was during these periods of retreat and reflection that I encountered Lloyd Blankfein and Goldman Sachs, the wreckers of Greece; the Koch brothers and their funding of libertarian and conservative causes through the Koch Industries foundations based in Wichita (Kansas); David Rockefeller and his family, founders of the Bilderberg Foundation, the Trilateral Commission, and heads of Chase Manhattan Bank; David Rubinstein's Carlyle Group, which did favors for the CIA; the old asset manager Fidelity, founded in 1946 by Boston pioneer Edward Johnson; the Vanguard investment fund created by John Bogle in 1975; and finally BlackStone, which would become BlackRock under Larry Fink. My masters of the world. I lived with them for twelve years.

When I hear statistics from Oxfam about the 1% of billionaires gaining more wealth each year, I think of these individuals, their stories, their origins, and how they maneuvered and bought politicians to build this global network and rotten situation, where it's impossible to dislodge them. Buying politicians, how scandalous! Most of our elected officials are honest... and so on. How many times have I heard this nonsense whenever I voiced my frustration? We now know, thanks to Julia Cagé's work, that La République en Marche was financed by a few hundred wealthy patrons who multiplied their tax-deductible donations of 7,500 euros by appealing to all family members. They were eager to see a president eliminate the ISF, thus allowing them to recover their investments. We saw how billionaire Marc Ladret de Lacharrière was generous with Pénélope and François Fillon, the right-wing presidential favorite. And what about those liberals like Laurent Wauquiez, who, as an election loomed, sought subsidies from traders at Goldman Sachs or Morgan Stanley: "These people support my political action and the sums were not large," Wauquiez justified.

So yes, some bourgeois, aristocrats, wealthy individuals, rentiers, and champions of finance buy politicians like one would buy a prostitute or a taxi. Am I too harsh? Try finding this Channel 4 report: a journalist disguises himself as a lobbyist and meets with Stephen Byers, an influential MP in the Commons, former Secretary of State for the Treasury and Transport under Tony Blair. The fake lobbyist explains he wants to pass a law favorable to his company. Byers names his price and agrees to campaign with his colleagues. He asks for 5,500 euros per day for the job and confesses, "I'm like a taxi, you can rent me." Jeff Bezos saw his fortune increase by 13 billion dollars in a single day, on July 20, 2020, despite the Covid crisis. That's the total value of Société Générale. Hypothetically, if we let Amazon thrive, Jeff Bezos, its owner, could become the first trillionaire in history within five years. A thousand billion dollars for one person…

I was trying to understand what was happening. Why did rich and well-endowed countries create so much poverty? I read articles on finance, watched videos, interviewed judges, bankers, financial journalists, politicians, lawyers, and police officers. My bedside books included works such as *Tous pouvoirs confus* (EPO, 2003) by Geoffrey Geuens and *La Finance imaginaire* by the same author (Aden, 2011). Their appendices contained endless lists of shareholders and board members of banks, trading companies, multinationals, and media. "Revealing all these intersecting networks of interests and collusions is to draw the true organizational chart of the globalization of the great powers. Indispensable for consciously entering into resistance," stated the back cover of the first book. In nearly twenty years, our resistance has not been very fierce, even if our conscience has been forged and hardened.

I made connections and wove webs. I searched for the men who hid behind the systems. Who held the keys to these routes, safes, investment funds, and offshore companies? Who decided on factory closures, bought media outlets, corrupted officials, or influenced films shown in town? Who determined our end-of-month spending and sought to privatize our pensions and social protections? How could one do journalism and publish original information in a world where everything seemed compromised? Could writing save me? Save us? What room did a journalist, writer, or editor have? These questions haunted me, and in the Abbesses studio, I imagined and constructed branching plans where these names I engraved in white oilcloth chalk on painted and repainted black backgrounds constantly recurred: Larry Fink, Lloyd Blankfein, Timothy Geithner, Frank Carlucci, David Rockefeller, the Koch brothers, and many others.

These paintings, drawings, and writings illustrate, accompany, and make up this book today. The more I read and questioned the power of finance, circling around the stars and rentiers of finance and American pension funds, the more I understood their intimate mechanisms. Money means little once you reach a certain threshold of wealth. It becomes exponential and unrelated to life, corrupting it and creating a paranoid relationship with others. Anyone can fall and pass to the other side. Getting rich, losing everything, or enjoying your money becomes inconsequential at a billion dollars. Wealth is never an end in itself. I think Larry understands that. His driving force is not merely to accumulate wealth but to hold power and continue growing relentlessly. You stop investing in that environment, and you die. You always bet last. The richer you are, the easier it is. And when you become too big to fail, that's good. If you fall, others fall with you. Larry Fink's multinational has become so vast that no one can measure its contours and roots. It is a galaxy, part of the air that the most important companies on the planet breathe.

Chapter 08

And so, I produced these canvases during the summer of 2012. There were thirty-one painted in about a month of reclusive life. Twenty-one canvases that follow one another and fit together, and about ten others that I designed as a special unit. I was possessed by this monomania of developing plans. My vision of power and earthly life. In many canvases – I realize it today – the name of Laurence Douglas Fink – known as Larry – came up again, as well as BlackRock, or BlackStone, its primitive version.

On black backgrounds, I made connections between the shareholders of investment funds and listed companies: Coca-Cola, Chevron, Pepsi, Exxon, Total, Axa, BNP Paribas, Siemens, Enron, General Electric, Merrill Lynch, Barclays, Vanguard, Fidelity, and BlackRock. I looked for money laundering cases that had appeared in the press, pinning the complicit banks and their offshore companies along the way. I added verbs like "eat, love, destroy, hide, take, steal." I slipped in phrases like "the art of ignoring the poor." A year later, at an exhibition, a collector told me about the artist Mark Lombardi and his plans and maps. Lombardi had gone from painting and drawing to making investigative journalism an art. And I was unknowingly taking the diametrically opposite path. After exhibiting in major American museums, Lombardi committed suicide in 2000. He was found hanged in his small Brooklyn studio, a month after the most significant exhibition of his career at the Whitney Museum in New York. He had shown his most monumental work: three and a half meters by one meter thirty-two. Value: five or six million euros...

The work he named BCCI-ICIC & FAB 1972-91 (4th version, 1996-2000) maps the bankruptcy of BCCI (Bank of Credit and Commerce International). It was a huge Anglo-Pakistani Islamist bank nicknamed "the bank of crime and corruption." The name of Osama Bin Laden was mentioned there, as well as his links with the Bush family. When I discovered his monumental canvas, it was an incredible shock for me. I knew the history of BCCI and its protagonists well, having covered it in a chapter of my first book on Clearstream. The Luxembourg firm had conducted transactions even after judicial authorities had ordered the accounts to be frozen. It was then the most resounding bank failure on the planet. Since then, Lehman Brothers has surpassed it. BCCI was present in seventy-three countries. The losses are estimated at nine billion dollars. All subsidiaries worldwide were closed on July 7, 1991. The origin of this bankruptcy lies in the discovery by the American DEA (Drug Enforcement Administration) of drug trafficking with Colombia. BCCI laundered the money of drug traffickers with the complicity of certain politicians.

After September 11, 2001, FBI agents took a serious look at Lombardi's work, spending days at the museum, photographing every scrap of canvas to reconstruct the terrorists' itinerary and financing. Lombardi used press articles and DEA reports, such as John Kerry's. He made connections that no one had dared to make before him. He was hyperlucid, meticulous, and obsessive. His driving force as an artist-journalist could be summed up as follows: everything we are looking for and that seems mysterious and unfindable is known, before our eyes. But too many media, political, or legal obstacles prevent us from seeing it.

So I am going to exhibit it. No one wants to see what I see. I see what no one sees. Look... I put on canvas, in museums or galleries, what no one reads in the newspapers anymore. I push the scandal to its paroxysm.

To create, if not to solve the problem, a work of art. A pure and uncorrupted object.

Lombardi had reached a point of no return. Let's say that halfway through this introspective and personal work, I came to the same conclusion. Especially since the BCCI bankruptcy was at the origin of the Clearstream scandal. It's all about ramifications.

Lombardi's death is shrouded in great mystery. Some, including those close to him, think he was murdered. Even his Wikipedia page casts doubt: "Mark Lombardi is an American contemporary artist born in Syracuse on March 23,

1951, and died on March 22, 2000, in New York, Williamsburg, officially by suicide."

I went back to follow Lombardi's footsteps in Brooklyn in 2013. My daughter lived there. I visited his neighborhood and met one of his friends. I wanted to write a book. And I gave up, caught up by life. Maybe I was afraid of what I was going to discover. I have a vague idea of the reasons for this suicide. Like any artist sacrificing himself to his art and his passion, Mark Lombardi got lost along the way. He told himself that his life had to become a work of art. And that only his death could allow it. Soaked in whiskey, lost in his thought patterns, he took the plunge, leaving behind troubled notes, a quantity of neatly arranged handwritten Bristol cards (fifteen thousand), and a messy workshop.

Mark Lombardi believed that he could compete with what did not yet exist. An artificial intelligence capable of interpreting so many connections. Aladdin. He must have had this premonition that everything he had undertaken for all these years was useless. The only way to give perspective to his work was to hang himself from a rope. And disappear.

Lombardi's diagrams were born out of the artist's insatiable curiosity about government scandals. For years, first as a researcher and then as a librarian in Houston, he meticulously documented the networks of alliances between the worlds of politics and finance on a global scale. His investigation led him in the footsteps of George Bush and Bill Clinton, through the closed circles of the Vatican, the Mafia, arms and drug trafficking, terrorism, and corruption. The works he produced from them draw the topography of a system of power, fueled by financial transactions and shaken by judicial convictions, over a period from the 1930s to the 1990s. One can enter Lombardi's drawings from any point on the map. The interaction of political, economic, and social forces takes the form of a complex network. The eye is spontaneously drawn to certain convergence nodes from which a concentration of lines radiates. These arcs point to secondary nodes, which rebound and unfold again to form the ramifications of a system of interconnected points. The space within which Lombardi locates these systems is relative, flexible, extensible...

The writer of these lines is a researcher at the Institut national de la recherche scientifique de Montréal. Her name is Nathalie Casemajor Loustau. May she be thanked.

Chapter 09

The names of Larry Fink and his BlackRock came back like a mantra. BlackRock and the BlackRockers: that's what they're called in financial circles. That's how they check each other out and co-opt each other. The tough guys. The Blacks. Nothing to do with hard rock or music. Larry, who created a record company called Octogone, is more of a fan of Californian music. He must have liked the Beach Boys. Octogone has now disappeared. Everything to do with the pride of being one and with a good dose of darkness, therefore cynicism.

In 2012, Larry was already almost everywhere. By 2020, he was everywhere. He had crushed all his competitors with his presence, thanks to factors that were not always under control. Larry Fink is alone in the world. He is the most informed man, or the most powerful man in the world. Larry Fink is, for a few more years, a discreet Master of the Universe. BlackRock is his cover. Aladdin his algorithm. And Heike Buchter the first biographer of his exploits. Heike, a journalist for *Die Zeit*, has lived in Manhattan for nineteen years and frequents Wall Street to gather information on the financial giants. She wrote her book on BlackRock in 2015 in German and has since updated it. A documentary directed by Tom Ockers, partly inspired by Heike's book, was broadcast on Arte in 2019. The fight against pension reform did the rest. We saw Larry and BlackRock appear on prime-time television news. The public learned that Jean-François Cirelli, former head of Gaz de France, now head of the French subsidiary of BlackRock, was decorated with the Legion of Honor by Emmanuel Macron. We saw Youth for Climate activists occupy the premises of the multinational's Parisian offices and get arrested by the police.

It should be noted that despite opportunistic speeches on the need to save the planet from global warming, BlackRock, a cold and schizophrenic entity, makes its investors a lot of money by financing the fossil fuel industry, thus contributing to environmental destruction. "Climate change is now a determining factor in the long-term prospects of companies," Larry writes in his annual letter at the start of 2020, addressed to the entrepreneurs with whom

BlackRock has dealings. "We will verify that companies are properly managing and monitoring these risks as part of their business. In the absence of precise reports, investors will be increasingly inclined to conclude that companies are not managing risks appropriately." Larry promises that in the future, he will vote "more readily against the management and directors of companies that are not making enough progress on sustainability reporting." Reports...

In an article in *Les Échos*, Lucie Pinson, spokesperson for Friends of the Earth, expresses her annoyance and deplores the fact that BlackRock is jumping on the bandwagon while continuing, through its investments in ETFs, listed funds, or shares in the oil or coal industry, to finance ultra-polluting mines or deposits: "The threshold chosen does not cover some of the largest coal producers, including more than a hundred companies planning new mines..."

The Davos forum, at the end of January 2020, was a grand moment of greenwashing. "Greta's best friend is finance!" headlined *La Tribune* on January 17, 2020. "In Davos, for the fiftieth edition of the World Economic Forum, activist Greta Thunberg will meet Donald Trump, but also Larry Fink, the boss of the BlackRock fund for whom 'climate risk has become a financial risk,'" explains its editorial director in an editorial. The latter had noted in a survey that, of the global risks seen by seven hundred and fifty business leaders, the top five concerns all related to the environment. The American star of the Forum, Larry strives to boast about his eco-friendly shift, thank Greta Thunberg, and explain to every microphone held out that he has had a sort of environmentalist revelation. Larry assures that everything will change, that sustainable investment has become the main lever for action. He promises transparency and commits to liquidating investments that show a high risk for the climate. "In his annual letter to his clients, 'Larry' also 'Greta,'" announces the editorial of *La Tribune*, "but with ringing and stumbling arguments: 'Climate risk has become a financial risk. In any case, in the world of finance, in which BlackRock is worth $7,500 billion, no one is burying their heads in the sand anymore. Companies, investors, and governments must prepare for a significant reallocation of capital in the near future, sooner than most people anticipate,' writes Larry Fink."

Transparency? An eco-friendly shift? The fight against global warming? In many complacent articles, I note that Larry plays it modestly, thriftily, and explains that he takes commercial planes for his travels and that he himself fights against global warming at his level. I was interested in Larry's recent trips to France. Five trips were recorded by civil aviation. We will return later to the purpose of these trips. All were made by private jet. And not just any jet: Gulfstreams. The Rolls-Royce of jets. Luxury planes with very high kerosene consumption. BlackRock owns three of them.

On board his Gulfstream G550 N3788B, Larry went to Paris on November 23, 2017, November 9, 2018, February 4, and March 15, 2019. His plane was purchased for $56 million in 2012 and consumes fifteen tons of fuel to travel eleven thousand kilometers.

Larry also bought a used Gulfstream G650 in December 2019, N1777M, with which he flew to Paris on January 20, 2020.

Finally, BlackRock bought a Gulfstream G600 in 2016, N10199, delivered on May 18, 2020. The plane has not yet left the USA. It is hidden under the name of the financial institution TVPX Aircraft and operated by a shell company, 2020 MSN 73021 Statutory Trust, Wyoming, according to the documents I was able to consult. The most interesting thing is their consumption. These long-haul business jets consume much more per passenger than well-filled wide-body aircraft: three liters per passenger for every hundred kilometers traveled for wide-body aircraft. Compared to twenty-eight liters per passenger for Larry's jet. In general, a Gulfstream G550 does not carry more than four passengers.

None of BlackRock's planes made any trips to France in 2015 and 2016. So, it was Emmanuel Macron's election that pushed Larry to come and breathe the air of Paris. And for a new convert to ecology, one can only be troubled by this gift of ubiquity and this propensity for greenwashing. Larry reminds me of a guy who would drive a Lamborghini Veneno and wear eco-friendly ethical cotton T-shirts with the "Join the Green Side" logo.

Chapter 10

We have heard many comments indicating that Larry Fink had influenced Emmanuel Macron to push through his pension reform. We saw a photo of Larry Fink with his employees and Emmanuel Macron in one of the salons of the Élysée, where the president received them discreetly.

In April 2020, the press, suddenly alert and concerned, reported that a subsidiary of BlackRock had won a call for tenders from the European Commission to advise its new leaders on climate matters.

The European Union Ombudsman, Emily O'Reilly, opened an investigation in July 2020 into this public contract awarded to BlackRock by the Commission. This investigation followed a complaint from eighty-four MEPs, mostly environmentalists, who were worried that the multinational, also responsible for auditing banks, was tasked with informing and monitoring the banking sector on integrating "environmental and social factors into their projects." Emily O'Reilly noted that "to win the contract, BlackRock submitted a proposal significantly lower than its seven competitors." BlackRock offered €280,000, while the other candidates' bids were closer to the ceiling of €500,000.

"It is not the gain on the service that interests the company, but the opportunity to participate, upstream, in defining the criteria for its future investments," Pascal Durand, MEP, ex-Green now Enmarcheur, explained to La Croix. The mix of genres is obvious for BlackRock: "Is the Commission aware that its decision leads to a conflict of interest where a company defines sectoral orientations that it will have to follow?" asked the MEPs. For Jean-Marc Jancovici, a climate expert quoted in the article: "The Commission has decided to entrust an American with the task of suggesting prudential rules for Europe, and to entrust an asset manager with the task of suggesting rules that will allow him to integrate 'sustainability', creating a significant conflict of interest." In a year, we have encountered BlackRock in many forms, without fully understanding what this sprawling financial company based in Manhattan was and how it operated. It suddenly seemed guilty of all evils and many words. The German book, translated for the first time into French and updated, filled this gap. The book is invigorating. The journalist takes us by the hand and tries, with anecdotes, short portraits, historical reminders, and pedagogy, to make the rise of BlackRock intelligible and to highlight the danger if we allow this firm with secret power to prosper unchecked.

I gave up on the idea of publishing my preface, not writing about it.

On May 12, on the Média.tv website, episode eight of my lockdown diary, "Assigned to Resistance," was titled "BlackRock is Watching You." An illustration showed Larry Fink as Big Brother. The editorial began like this: "While we deal with the epidemic, we forget that BlackRock is a virus just as dangerous in the long term, eroding our lives, our privacy, and our bank accounts. And it works in the shadows. BlackRock prospers like the mafia. The less we talk about it, the more it acts. And Larry Fink, the sixty-eight-year-old boss with the smooth demeanor of a clergyman, is a godfather who hides his game to better pick our pockets..."

In hindsight, and considering the attitude of the German publisher and the author of the book, I wonder if they read this text and misinterpreted it. I am not claiming that Larry is a mafia member or that BlackRock is an offshoot of Cosa Nostra. I am using a metaphor whose subtlety may have escaped our German friends.

Florent hesitates between publishing a book that gets off to a bad start and launching a tedious legal battle to claim all or part of the money invested in the publication and translation of the book.

Since I have no direct contact with the agent, the publisher, and the author, I sent Florent a letter addressed to them, indicating that I intend to write about BlackRock and that their refusal to publish my preface will be an integral part of this story.

At the time of writing this letter, I am not certain it will be a book, even though I feel that the material is there. And I don't have a publisher yet. I vaguely discussed it with my friend and publisher Bernard Barrault, who published my previous novels (Les Rapports humains, 2017) and my investigation into Charlie Hebdo (Mohicans, Julliard, 2015), but Bernard is not available for the start of the 2020 school year, as he is leaving Julliard to create a new publishing house. I tell myself that finding a publisher is not the issue. I want to write first. To do that, I need time. I will have some in August. The decision for Florent to publish the book will not come until September 2020, after reading the first lines. Quite naturally...

Dear Heike, dear German publisher,

When Florent Massot told me that you did not want my preface because – if I understood correctly – it went further than the book and could raise legal issues, I initially thought it was a joke. But no, you really thought that. Needless to say, I am used to these questions, and my preface does not contain any defamation or pose any legal problem.

Apart from the rudeness of condemning a work that was commissioned and planned for a long time without explanation, I would like to understand what motivates you. Is there a specific paragraph or word that I missed?

Is Heike afraid that I will overshadow her promotion? If that is the case, I am ready to hear it, but it seems far-fetched to me and is a misunderstanding of my work. The preface would have undoubtedly helped to promote the book. Perhaps my reputation? The numerous lawsuits I have had and won against Clearstream, whose parent company is German? Is she aware of my legal victories? That said, I really don't see how this preface wouldn't benefit the book and its sales. But maybe you don't want the book to succeed in France? Perhaps you're worried that my involvement will harm your relationships with Wall Street financiers who are surely sources that could dry up? Or maybe you're concerned about your job as a journalist and correspondent for a prominent title in Germany?

I'm lost in conjecture. I'd like you to answer my questions, which are motivated not by animosity or hurt pride but by a genuine desire to understand. My question is journalistic and serious.

I will write about BlackRock and inform my readers of what must be called the censorship of this preface. It is unfortunate since your book, although somewhat dated, is invigorating. I learned things about Larry Fink, Aladdin, and the construction of BlackRock by reading it. I had and have no malicious intent toward you.

In short, dear Heike, dear German publisher, thank you for considering my letter as questions posed by a journalist to another journalist and her publisher. Your answer – or refusal to answer me – will be part of the story and the investigation I plan to write this summer on BlackRock.

Fascinating subject that requires rigor and freedom.

Yours.

I sent this letter to Florent Massot on July 15, asking him to forward it to Heike Buchter via her agent. He sent it to his German contacts on August 14. He delayed because he was unsure whether he was going to publish Heike's book, and she was procrastinating. As of writing, I believe he still does not know.

Chapter 11

BlackRock no longer has major shareholders as it did until May 2020, when the largest, a major bank in Pittsburgh, sold its stakes. Its capital now belongs to a multitude of shareholders, including its competitor Vanguard, which owns more than 5%, as well as a major Kuwaiti investment company and other American, Japanese, or Chinese fund managers. At the end of 2019, the group managed nearly $7,500 billion and employed 16,200 people across 30 countries. BlackRock provides advice and invests its clients' money in companies in around 100 countries, mainly in America and Europe. The Asian market, representing 10% of its activities, offers bright prospects. Despite these figures and the evolutionary curve of its gains, the firm keeps a low profile and downplays its resounding success. Larry Fink wants to be impenetrable, speaking only through the group's management.

Larry Fink, who is better informed about the state of the financial world and therefore more powerful than Warren Buffett, Bill Gates, Mark Zuckerberg, or Tim Cook combined, wants to appear as a normal guy dedicated to the growth, profit, and prosperity of his clients. He portrays himself as the anti-Gordon Gekko, the Wall Street character played by Michael Douglas in Oliver Stone's film where "money never sleeps." Unlike Larry, who aims to pass for the average American, he is portrayed as having a simple lifestyle: pajamas, herbal tea, and in bed by 10 p.m.—no coke, no alcohol, no vice.

In her book, Heike Buchter depicts Larry as a monochromatic figure, reflecting the financial press's portrayal of him. This image aligns with the one that the most influential man on Wall Street wants to project. Larry's success is attributed to his businessman father's education in Los Angeles, where he learned the trade of shoe salesman at age ten. This narrative was repeated on television during his last visit to Davos. After brilliant studies, he entered the bank with the fervor of an evangelist. At First Boston, he achieved major successes until a disastrous loss of $100 million due to a lack of foresight on the real estate market. This initial setback proved to be foundational. Larry joined BlackStone in 1988, a New York investment fund, where he headed the risk unit. That year, Larry's benefactors were two prominent bankers: Stephen Schwarzman and Pete Peterson. Both were right-wing Republicans with libertarian tendencies. Peterson had been Secretary of Commerce under Nixon, and Schwarzman, who compared Obama to Hitler during a 2010 shareholders' meeting over a tax increase proposal, is a Trump supporter known for lavish spending, such as hiring Rod Stewart for his birthday.

The two billionaires provided Larry with a $5 million advance to start his fund. They took a 50% stake in what they called BFM (BlackStone Financial Management) and offered the remaining 50% to Larry and his team. The origin of the name BlackRock reflects Schwarzman's surname, "Schwartz" (black in German), leading to "Black" in BlackStone and then BlackRock, and Peterson's first name "Peter" contributing to "Rock."

Larry had vision and tenacity but lacked imagination. In 1988, fresh from his failure at First Boston, he did not foresee that he would later name his company BlackRock and achieve significant success. The inevitable breakup with Schwarzman seemed likely, but it might have been feigned. According to well-placed sources, Schwarzman, nicknamed "Schwarzy the Crazy," might still support Larry behind the scenes. The legend of Larry as a solitary banker struggles against the reality of Wall Street, where alliances are crucial. Larry needed support to facilitate BlackRock's massive expansion and make it acceptable to investment bankers and private equity champions.

In a rare 2010 interview with CNBC, Larry reflected on his biggest mistake, attributing it to not having enough confidence to start his own investment company in risk management. He praised Schwarzman and Peterson for their belief in him and their investment decision.

By 1994, Larry was ready to break free from his sponsors, leading to strained relations. He persuaded Pittsburgh bank PNC (Pittsburgh National City) to invest $240 million to buy out Schwarzman and Peterson's shares. Schwarzman, going through a divorce, needed cash and would later regret this decision. With PNC as a quiet partner holding 25% of the shares, Larry was free to upscale and invest in risk management, including the creation of

Aladdin. Larry relied on Rob Kapito, a friend from First Boston, and was supported by a diverse board of directors, including members from Mexico, the UK, Kuwait, Canada, and major corporations. Notably absent were Europeans.

Kapito remains at BlackRock, unlike PNC Financial, which sold its shares in May 2020 for $14.4 billion (22.4% of BlackRock's capital). This sale was surprising as PNC had previously valued its shares at $17 billion. The buyers included a Singaporean sovereign fund, a Kuwaiti sovereign fund, and various existing BlackRock shareholders, such as Vanguard, State Street, Fidelity, and Capital Group.

The sale was driven by concerns that American banking authorities might classify BlackRock as a subsidiary of PNC, which Larry wanted to avoid. He sought to maintain BlackRock's status as an independent asset manager, avoiding regulatory scrutiny and maintaining flexibility. BlackRock's role as a fund management platform is complemented by its advisory and investment services, with Aladdin playing a key role. This positions BlackRock similarly to platforms like Uber, Blablacar, or Amazon, managing global capital without borders. As of December 2019, amid criticism from environmental activists and political figures in France over its influence on pension reform, BlackRock issued a statement emphasizing its role as an independent asset manager not involved in pension funds directly.

Larry's obsession is to avoid being classified as a bank, preferring the status of an "independent asset manager" to evade regulatory scrutiny. His preference for maintaining this status reflects his desire to avoid the constraints and oversight associated with banking.

Chapter 12

In the documentary by Tom Ockers, broadcast by Arte in September 2019, titled "These Financiers Who Run the World," an archive perfectly illustrates the danger posed by BlackRock and Larry Fink's solitary and expansionist management. In July 2016, on a CNBC show, which is a friendly and rather institutional television program where clashes are rare, Larry Fink, dressed in a dark blue suit, long silk tie, and gold glasses, is seated on a couch next to hedge fund manager Carl Icahn, a very rich old wolf of Wall Street. You have to be wary of old wolves, especially when they are rich, as they sometimes feel invincible and forget conventions.

Faced with a Larry Fink who is increasingly incredulous and shrinking, Carl Icahn says, with a hint of amusement: "I believe that BlackRock is an extremely dangerous company. And I am serious." He then uses a metaphor to describe the country's financial situation and the role of BlackRock: "We're like a disco bus where everyone is having a drink. They're all there having fun. And you know who's pushing it? Larry Fink and Janet Yellen are driving. They're the ones pushing this damned shack." Icahn accuses Fink and Yellen, on this show widely watched by executives and managers, of knowingly risking a new financial crisis. He goes further, suggesting that while the Fed chair seems momentarily aware of the danger, Larry, in a sort of reckless and self-destructive drunkenness, is pushing everyone to make mistakes and crash: "This bus is on its way, and Janet tries from time to time to slow it down. Janet is worried and Larry doesn't agree; he wants to let the party continue and the party-goers shout: 'No! Don't brake!' We're having a blast!" And they're heading straight for a cliff. And the bus is heading... This bus is going to plunge, and at the end there's a cliff and you know what it's going to crash into? A black rock... A black rock."

They are going to hit a black rock.

Carl is laughing. Larry, less so.

Everyone on the CNBC set is laughing, except for the BlackRock boss, who mumbles a few sentences to say that he does not have, and cannot have, control over financial markets that could get out of control: "They are controlled by everyone who participates in them." Curtain.

It's a stunning sequence because, in two minutes, we are confronted with a harsh truth. It's TV, I know. But precisely, television, especially American television, and particularly on a channel like CNBC, which is often benevolent towards money and the powerful, makes the exchange even more delicious, improbable, and disturbing. One billionaire faces another. One is a rentier, a user of the system, a person for whom the end of the month tastes the same as the end of a century. The other is a player in the system, a living god of the back office, the son of a poor man. The billionaire expresses his concern about seeing the hard-working man screw up the system. The billionaire is old. We can hope he has no worries about his future. No, he just tells us that right now, it sucks... It really sucks to leave the keys to the truck to Larry... He went on television to get this message across. The system on which capitalism was built, which enriched it but also kept the poor on a leash, is perhaps taking a path with no other exit than a leap into the void if we leave a guy like Larry at the wheel.

What can Larry do, apart from smiling foolishly and saying that everything is fine and under control?

Everything in his attitude, gestures, and words betrays his great embarrassment and expresses the opposite.

The film continues with Stefan Walter, the CEO of the ECB: "Banks must have more equity; before the crisis, they had perhaps 8 or 9% on average. Today, they have between 13 and 14% in the eurozone. This is an average; the figures can vary."

We are reassured.

BlackRock today handles much more money than most banks, but the multinational is much less controlled: since it is not a banking institution and does not grant credits, it is not considered to be of systemic importance. Let's not be afraid to say that BlackRock is out of control. Out of touch. Far from the world of the living, of workers, of the economy. BlackRock is nothing but speculation.

Stefan Walter continues: "We say that an institution is systemically important when it is likely, in the event of difficulty, to cause a shock in the financial system that could have negative consequences for the real economy."

The guy is the head of the ECB. He weighs every word carefully. A shock? Negative consequences?

We are less reassured. Let's not forget that the expression "too big to fail" was invented for banks and multinationals. It does not mean that banks or multinationals are immovable and cannot fall. On the contrary, it means that they can, but if such an outcome were to occur, the entire system would collapse. These banks would bring down dozens of other banks and companies with them. After all, dinosaurs were also too big to disappear.

Let us recall a quote from Alan Greenspan, then head of the Fed, who had more humor than the current head of the ECB: "If you think you understood what I said, it's because I expressed myself badly."

Suddenly, I feel better.

François Morin, an economist from Toulouse, has remarkably studied the phenomenon, which he considers imminent, of a systemic crisis. He particularly focused on the thirty or so so-called "systemic" banks (four of which are French), because they are too big to be controlled and all interconnected. "All it takes is for one of them to lose the confidence of the others, and the entire global financial system collapses," he warns.

Unless, as in 2008, central banks or illicit money comes to save the banking system. The banking crisis was so severe that even the Swiss Federal Council was forced to rescue UBS, whose shares had collapsed. There was only one source of money available on a global scale that could provide international banks with a breath of fresh air: drug money. This is what Antonio Maria Costa, the UN executive director in charge of the fight against drugs and crime, explained in a now-famous report. All intelligence agencies turned a blind eye to the laundering of $352 billion from Mexican cartels. The American bank Wachovia, a subsidiary of Wells Fargo, which served as an intermediary, was fined a mere $162 million.

Following the reasoning and information provided by Tom Ockers' witnesses, we get lost along the way and sink into the dark. The risk of a systemic crisis here would be based on the presence of too many ETFs sold by BlackRock.

Larry's firm operates with what traders call OPM (Other People's Money): pension funds, insurance companies, and small savers. This is an additional element that differentiates Carl Icahn and Larry. Carl considers that the money he earned (among other things, thanks to Larry's tools—$15 billion, all the same) is his own. Larry, the son of a shoe merchant and a teacher, will always play, even at BlackRock, with other people's money.

Starting with around ten million dollars invested, BlackRock provides personalized advice. Below that amount, for the smallest investors, BlackRock offers its new, flagship, affordable, and popular "product" among stock market speculators from all countries: these strange financial objects called ETFs.

How far will BlackRock go?

Larry has built his reputation and success on these exchange-traded funds. In reality, he does not negotiate anything; he imposes. These collective funds are the latest discovery of Wall Street bankers and traders that Larry has embraced. Instead of buying an individual stock or bond, you buy a lot with an index. This is new—since 2009—and ETFs are going to be big money. "At BlackRock, we are like at an Italian ice cream parlor," explains Heike Buchter in his book.

We have dozens of flavors and colors. We can sell our clients an investment in the French CAC 40, in biochemistry, in electric cars, in Norwegians, in oil, armaments, wind energy, soft drinks. We choose what we like and we buy. BlackRock will very quickly become the global supermarket of ETFs, the largest provider of exchange-traded funds in the world. Remember, we no longer buy an individual share but a basket of various shares grouped under a value, a stock market index. BlackRock will, for example, more readily sell you €10,000 of ETF grouping CAC 40 shares than €10,000 of Total shares...

BlackRock takes care of everything... If the CAC 40 rises, the BlackRock index rises in the same way. The same applies in the event of a fall. No one decides which shares to buy anymore. The ETF tracks the value of BlackRock's selection that makes up the index.

According to the documentary, these ETFs make up a third of the company's assets. BlackRock's success is largely due to this brilliant and formidable invention.

Just before the sequence with Larry, Robin Wigglesworth, a journalist from the Financial Times, acknowledges that BlackRock, because of these ETFs, needs to be better monitored. Philippe Escande, an economic journalist at Le Monde, joins him and admits that BlackRock is either ignored or too little known by the public.

It's not much, but it's a start. Without wishing to underestimate the quality of my colleagues (we share a press card), I share the opinion of Ernest Backes, my first informant in the Clearstream affair, who never stopped repeating to me: "Financial journalism does not exist; there are only journalists paid by the banks." Backes was probably exaggerating.

Chapter 13

In June 2009, while the aftermath of the subprime crisis kept the world in suspense, BlackRock acquired the investment subsidiary of the stricken British bank Barclays for $13.5 billion—a colossal transaction. Overnight, BlackRock saw its assets double. More worryingly, the company began marketing highly popular and affordable ETFs under the iShares brand, which quickly came to constitute a third of BlackRock's assets. ETFs gained immense popularity. Since the financial crisis, stock market speculators, who have become the cash cows of the system, have lost trust in banks and are seeking more profitable and transparent investment solutions, especially since savings accounts yield little. In the United States, ETFs have become all the rage. The Arte documentary highlights this, with Robin Wigglesworth of the Financial Times stating: "BlackRock is the biggest provider of ETFs. This has allowed us all to save at a lower cost. But the enormous pressure this has created has forced asset managers to lower their prices. Last year, the price of these services fell to a historically low level: half what it was twenty years ago. Everyone has made huge savings."

Here, let's be honest—the journalist is defending ETFs. However, this reasoning is tautological. It's remarkable how these journalists, stuck in their roles and salaries, claim to represent everyone, including those who are financially struggling. But what if everyone decided to sell their ETFs? Who would save the system?

Christopher R. Whalen, a witness in the documentary and a Wall Street banker, is unsure. It seems evident that a management company like BlackRock does not have sufficient reserves or equity in the event of a disaster.

We then move to Canada, where David Schumacher, a key witness in the Arte documentary and an assistant professor of financial economics at McGill University, has published a study titled *Who is Afraid of BlackRock?* in collaboration with two other researchers. They advocate for the regulation of all financial institutions. The film shows that if everyone panicked and sold their ETFs simultaneously, the financial system would suffer and become unstable, or even more so. The buyer would save the system. If you sell the CAC 40 index, you are likely to find a price that reflects its new value, even if it falls. All markets fluctuate according to the law of supply and demand. This is true for ETFs just as it is for any commercial product.

Can the ETF system implode? The system has set up "circuit breakers," which are downward (and upward) thresholds at which transactions stop to allow operators to assess the market and return to normal operation. A security can collapse in the event of bankruptcy, but an index reflecting a panel of leading stocks, representative of the French economy for example, is less likely to implode or collapse. Unless—regarding the CAC 40—France is wiped off the map, but that's another story.

Not all ETFs have the stability of the CAC 40. Who will buy ETFs if they start plunging? Good question.

A former BlackRock employee, who spoke anonymously in San Francisco, expressed fears of prosecution by the multinational. It feels like being immersed in a documentary on Scientology, with Larry Fink resembling Ron Hubbard. The employee explained that there was immense pressure at BlackRock to sell ETFs to clients. BlackRock and Vanguard, its main shareholder, dominate two-thirds of the market for these new-style stock portfolios. Shares in these companies are rising.

Millions of Americans, influenced by advertising, invest their retirement savings in ETFs, expecting BlackRock to secure their future pensions.

You need to watch this documentary several times, as it can be confusing in places, to understand its implications and underlying messages. In a Californian court, a strange trial is underway—BlackRock against its employees. The company is accused of transferring employees' pension money to obscure funds and collecting fees on each transaction, neglecting the capital interests of its employees to boost profits. The former employee remarks: "It is likely that

BlackRock will drag out the proceedings for years, and I will not receive a cent. BlackRock has failed in its obligations."

On September 3, 2019, U.S. District Judge Haywood S. Gilliam Jr. dismissed, in large part, BlackRock's requests against its employees' class action, so the case continues.

Larry? Any comments?

BlackRock is a major player. Even the cautious Christopher R. Whalen acknowledges: "BlackRock is so significant that it influences the market." Similarly, Steven Davidoff Solomon, a law professor at Berkeley, notes: "BlackRock is the linchpin of the financial markets. They have an enormous responsibility."

The director seems apprehensive about lawsuits and struggles to draw a clear moral. However, towards the end of the film, a witness provides the key insight: BlackRock consolidates the system and "makes the rich even richer." What a surprise!

Chapter 14

BlackRock, without the mastery and omnipotence of Aladdin, is nothing.

Heike Buchter's book sheds light on how BlackRock transitioned from a prosperous company to the leading force in the underworld of business: the subprime crisis of 2008. The episode recounted by Katrina Brooker, a journalist from *Fortune*, is revealing. On September 15, Larry Fink left Wall Street for an overseas trip. After a ten-hour flight, he learned the unthinkable: Lehman Brothers had gone bankrupt, erased from existence. Merrill Lynch was sold to Bank of America, and AIG, the once-dominant insurer, was faltering. "I felt like Charlton Heston on the Planet of the Apes," Larry Fink tells the journalist with unusual humor.

In the futuristic film inspired by Pierre Boulle's French novel, an astronaut played by Charlton Heston believes he has landed on a distant planet populated by fighting apes. At the end of his journey, he discovers the ruins of the Statue of Liberty, realizing that humanity has destroyed Earth and its civilization has vanished.

"For Fink and his team, it was the beginning of a transformation. From an asset manager with a preference for bonds and intelligent analysts, they became one of the major players behind the scenes of high finance and high politics," writes Heike Buchter. In October 2008, in the aftermath of the subprime disaster, lost and uncertain, the US Treasury Department and the Federal Reserve called on Larry Fink and BlackRock to help sort through AIG's accounts, distinguishing between healthy and toxic securities. Thanks to his network of political connections—bridging Wall Street and Washington, D.C.—and his reputation as a risk management supercomputer, Larry Fink proved indispensable. He accepted all missions entrusted to him, particularly untangling the 2008 crash, tracking down corrupt credits, and preventing the crisis from deepening. This mission was awarded without a formal tender. "We didn't have time; we were in a hurry," the White House would justify. Larry's calculating skills and opportunism helped Obama save Citigroup, the leading American bank, by determining the amount to be invested.

On November 23, 2008, following a drop in Citigroup's stock price by about 70%, the American federal government guaranteed more than $300 billion of its assets in exchange for a $27 billion stake in the company. Obama paid without question by printing money.

"The story of BlackRock is the story of a reversal of power on Wall Street," says Heike Buchter.

Under Larry's leadership, the multinational conquered the world through consulting and investment. Between these two activities, Larry Fink, whose brain is almost superhuman, promised to have established a "Chinese wall"—a term BlackRockers swear by. According to Larry, there is a watertight partition between the advisory and investment activities of BlackRock. In other words, those whom the company advises on investment do not benefit from the information of those who manage the accounts. Even if, often, the same people are involved.

We must take his word for it, as no serious and independent investigation has ever been conducted on BlackRock, a sprawling firm that has become so influential that it is rarely questioned.

And then, a simple and consequential question arises: where will BlackRock go next?

Chapter 15

In an interview in the early 1990s, Larry Fink acknowledged that sometimes IT tools, by creating value, "can get out of control and become uncontrollable." He should revisit this observation today because, even for the cautious Heike Buchter, these IT tools are the main problem and growing danger hanging over our heads.

To win the game and dominate the markets in the long term, long before the advent of big data, Larry Fink created Aladdin, his IT behemoth that may one day replace humans—and potentially turn against them. I'm not being delusional here; it's Larry himself who fears and predicts this.

But to achieve this dominance by Aladdin and Larry in the financial markets, it was necessary to have IT expertise, infrastructure capable of calculating indices, securing them, and making them reliable for customers. This is where Aladdin and Larry's vision find their purpose and value.

Aladdin is an artificial intelligence. It stands for Asset, Liability, Debt, and Derivative Investment Network. Aladdin was born out of Larry Fink's deep-seated paranoia about risk. He set up his giant computers, which are constantly processing data, in Wenatchee, on the banks of the Columbia River, four thousand kilometers from New York, in an Indian territory in the northern United States where, due to numerous dams, electricity is the cheapest in the country. For centuries, the Wanapum tribe lived along the banks in reed huts, subsisting on salmon fishing. European settlers gradually took over the land, and engineers built dams that blocked the salmon's annual migration. Today, the last descendants of the Wanapum live in modest houses built by the electric company. Electricity providers have been operating the four hundred dams on the Columbia and its tributaries since the 1950s. What deprived the Native Americans of their way of life has laid the groundwork for a new industry in the Columbia Basin: data centers.

Heike Buchter's book teaches us that, through the rise of BlackRock, a broader history of America unfolds. She looks back at how large American corporations, after World War II, became convinced they could dominate both domestic and international markets, only to fall victim to the Chinese "ogre" that partly devoured them. Globalization led to the decline of giants like General Motors, and companies increasingly sought to evade their social responsibilities. Ronald Reagan, during his presidency, did significant damage by privatizing American retirement savings. He was followed by Maggie Thatcher in the UK. François Mitterrand, although initially resistant to privatization, eventually yielded to Jacques Delors and the banking lobby over Pierre Mauroy and the Communists. The rest is history.

In the U.S., the Republican administration promoted individual retirement savings plans through capitalization, shifting the responsibility of economic hardship from employers to employees. This policy, focused on reducing state intervention, public debt, and taxes while increasing entrepreneurial freedom, has led to a situation where pockets are increasingly empty and children are hungry. This speculative system, advocated by Larry and his ilk, is heading towards a critical point.

Thanks to the influences on Ronald Reagan, including the Rockefellers and others, new American employee savings plans were opened to the stock market. Active capitalists—owners of capital, bosses, big shareholders, and their supporters—claim that more government means more public debt, thus transferring costs to future generations. But this is misleading. They have little concern for future generations.

Initially, the system may appear successful, like a Ponzi scheme that brings in more and more, but eventually, it breaks and becomes catastrophic. This is the current reality, thirty years after Reagan's policies. American workers' savings have shifted to retirement investment funds, managed by financial companies and prominent investment banks like Fidelity, Pimco, Vanguard, Blackstone, and BlackRock. This rise of fund managers is pivotal.

Returning to the Columbia River, the digital industry seeks to minimize its largest expense: energy. BlackRock, along with banks, financial companies with their sleek buildings on the Hudson, and tech giants like Yahoo, Microsoft, and Dell, have established their servers near Wenatchee.

Strange irony: the Native Americans are still being deprived. The digital and financial barons' computers, though imposing, are smaller and less energy-hungry than Larry's. The lines of code in Aladdin's program are unparalleled, except perhaps by those of Facebook and its billions of users.

Aladdin grows continuously, fed by new data. As with Google and other tech companies, this data is provided voluntarily by users—primarily large investors. Aladdin knows where capital flows globally and where it originates. Even ordinary consumer data can find its way to Aladdin. Hundreds of people have worked on Aladdin's programs for over two decades. Aladdin now consists of an army of thousands of analysts and about six thousand computers, performing hundreds of millions of calculations per week—a facility that would make NASA envious.

In 2019, the values administered by Aladdin were estimated at $18 trillion. By 2020, this figure had surpassed $21.5 trillion. The system has no apparent limits.

The danger lies in the financial world's reliance on Aladdin. BlackRock should consider spinning off its AI, as Aladdin should be clearly separated from BlackRock to mitigate systemic risk.

Chapter 16

When BlackRock won the European Commission's environmental consulting competition, it probably owed its success—though no one has pointed this out—to Aladdin. The Commission bought Larry's speed and AI diagnostics.

BlackRock advises the Fed, the ECB, Airbus, Exxon, JPMorgan, and Apple. Heike Buchter reports:

"Central banks are very interesting clients; they have valuable information, especially for market players. Because no one can control markets like they do. Yes, of course, there are the famous 'Chinese walls,' organizational precautions meant to prevent employees from knowing what they shouldn't. But when you mention 'Chinese walls' on Wall Street, you usually get a smile and a shrug in return."

For French companies alone, BlackRock owns 6.3% of Total, 6.5% of Sanofi, 6.4% of Publicis, 5.9% of Danone, 6% of Schneider, 5% of BNP Paribas, 2.74% of Peugeot, 1.9% of LVMH, and 4.97% of Pernod Ricard. BlackRock votes at the general meetings of seventeen thousand companies worldwide.

Until recently, BlackRock, aware of its status as a passive shareholder, had refrained from intervening in power games—a tacit but immutable rule. However, this situation changed in 2020. Between January and June, BlackRock took positions opposed to the prevailing powers at about half of the general meetings where it could vote.

Every year, at Davos, where he is a key figure, Larry Fink writes to shareholders of the companies in which BlackRock invests, using cryptic language and rarely making a bold statement. "Every company must contribute positively to society," he declared this year.

By investing widely, BlackRock ends up with stakes in both competitive and overlapping properties. For example, BlackRock owns 1% of Adidas and 3% of Puma, and it is a shareholder in many competing airlines.

This is a common issue for funds that invest in specific sectors. It is not unusual for funds to pick stocks in a given area. For some, BlackRock's presence, even as a small minority shareholder, becomes a mark of recognition—part of the "BlackRock club." Conversely, when Larry Fink or Warren Buffett decide to sell, even for simple profit-taking, all other shareholders become apprehensive. Larry Fink, at 68, is relatively young compared to Warren Buffett, who is 90. Like in politics, there is no age limit or intelligence test to ride a global financial giant. Warren Buffett alone can make a $91 billion line on Apple without adhering to diversification rules. "Diversification is a protection against ignorance," he argues. "It doesn't make much sense if you know what you're doing."

Common ownership is the rule, not the exception. Four funds—Vanguard, State Street, Fidelity, and BlackRock—are the majority shareholders in the five hundred largest American companies.

This surrender of authority to Wall Street banks is pitiful. Sovereignists can criticize this, but they are unable to resist it unless they question the notion of ownership. But that is another long story.

"Property is theft," said Pierre-Joseph Proudhon, who added, "Property and society are things that are invincibly repugnant to each other: it is as impossible to associate two owners as it is to make two magnets join by their similar poles. Either society must perish or it must kill property."

BlackRock also invests heavily in the airline sector, where non-compete agreements have led to an 11% increase in ticket prices, as shown in Tom Oakes' documentary. Martin Schmalz, a German researcher from Oxford, has questioned this management, which harms consumers for the benefit of shareholders. He was heard in 2018 by the Federal Trade Commission in New York. BlackRock has refused to respond to his accusations. That day, Barbara Novick, BlackRock's vice-president, was forced to defend the company: "Abandoning common ownership by limiting investment to one company per sector would make owning diversified portfolios impossible. However, this commitment is crucial in the chain of responsibility. It benefits both shareholders and society as a whole," she stated in front of Arte's cameras. It primarily benefits BlackRock... No one had the courage to tell her that her defense was inadequate.

BlackRock seems untouchable. Larry Fink has created a duopoly with his competitor Vanguard. Together, they manage 66% of the income from funded pensions in the US and 50% in Europe (where they are still a small minority).

They seek more. Hence the connections forged in France with Emmanuel Macron. In the Arte documentary, a former employee of BlackRock's San Francisco subsidiary, who is afraid to testify openly, described being pressured to convince clients to buy ETFs. The goal was to make BlackRock and its shareholders "richer and richer." Through these undifferentiated share purchases, he also increased the value of the companies in which BlackRock invested. Did he enrich his clients? Not always. His role was to make them believe in the stock market product's quality and reliability. Often, BlackRock's clients do not know what they are actually buying.

Heike Buchter translates this well in her book: "The sole objective of private equity is to increase the profit of the owners. Whether jobs are created or eliminated is only a side effect." She illustrates financial surrealism: "In financial capitalism 2.0, the link between owners and companies has become an ever-longer chain. The intermediate links are professional administrators acting on behalf of real investors. This phenomenon is known as the 'separation of ownership from control'... It sounds like a reference to Magritte, who wrote 'This is not a pipe' under an image of a pipe."

Proudhon partly predicted and denounced this almost two centuries ago: "In itself, property is a power of selfishness, which drives man, if he encounters no impediment, to appropriate everything around him, including men and things, and to assert his domination over the universe."

BlackRock faces very few obstacles in its strategy for financial domination and will face even fewer as Aladdin becomes the search engine for finance and the BlackRock platform. Larry is no longer hiding his stance. He warned his world, particularly the French, through a premonitory article by Sophie Fay in L'Obs: "Before leaving, Larry the technophile gives a little advice to Europeans: don't fear technology, take inspiration from Silicon Valley, an alliance of universities, entrepreneurs, and finance. He has partnered with Google to use more artificial intelligence in information analysis. His financial management company is gradually becoming a software company. Within five years, he predicts that selling the Aladdin platform—a solution allowing clients to have a clear view of their risks in real-time and even to automate their management—will represent 30% of his turnover. Moreover, on Wall Street, computers are rapidly replacing financiers in suspenders." Five years. By the spring of 2022. Time is running out…

A major downturn on Wall Street and at BlackRock may be imminent…

"Isn't this automation of finance dangerous in the long term?" a journalist asks. Larry's response, all smiles: "Technology improves financial knowledge and skills… Technology does not replace humans; that's a myth. But those who refuse to adapt will be swept away by those who seize it."

In two years, according to these forecasts, Aladdin will be the best friend of stockbrokers, savers, and pensioners. And Larry, if no one intervenes, will be the king of investors. He will likely triple his salary and surpass the entire clique of Wall Street bankers. Perhaps he will even enter the Forbes ranking of the hundred richest men on the planet.

"You want to secure your future, welcome to BlackRock, which presents Aladdin, the genie of stock market capitalization. Enter the amount of your investments in the blue box and trust us." Let's go.

Chapter 17

States, across all continents, seem to have capitulated to the omnipotence of BlackRock. By testing the resistance of American or European banks, on public or central bank orders, Aladdin has almost unlimited access to sensitive information.

On several occasions, its leaders have been suspected of insider trading, as in Greece or Ireland, at the time of buyouts of companies that BlackRock had audited. Or in Mexico, where President López Obrador, after an interview with Larry Fink, renounced the nationalization of Pemex, the oil company, and the abandonment of an oil pipeline between Mexico and Texas where BlackRock had interests and clients.

Larry knows how to surround himself wherever he invests. He hired the son of Mexican billionaire Carlos Slim and poached one of Pemex's board members from the Mexican pension fund manager for BlackRock.

It is only in Berlin that Larry has given in. After buying Deutsche Wohnen, a real estate company, at a rather high price, he wanted to increase rents but had to backtrack. In the summer of 2019, faced with the anger and mobilization of Berliners, street protests, the union of the so-called "radical" left and environmentalists, and even city council members who were devoted to BlackRock, rents were frozen for five years. The real estate company's stock fell by 20%. Larry was unhappy about it, but he quickly absorbed this loss in his monstrous accounting.

BlackRock has become the largest investor on the planet—by far. But the firm is less controlled than a bank, because it is not considered systemically important. We can see in this strangeness a new and serious danger.

For BlackRock, the permanent objective—its reason for being—is to continue winning markets and subsidies, bringing even more money from investors into their funds. The proximity of BlackRock executives to politicians opens up infinite possibilities. Larry is very adept at seducing them. He is BlackRock's best ambassador. By drawing inspiration from the methods used by close bankers, such as Jamie Dimon, CEO of JPMorgan Chase, the highest-paid banker on Wall Street, he has built up a network and effective strategies. For example, he explains that he is a Democrat but continues to sit on the entrepreneur commissions set up by Trump and the Republicans. He calls himself a Democrat, but he has never opposed the destruction of the Dodd-Frank Act, the founding act of the Trump presidency. Christopher Dodd and Barney Frank, both Democrats, carried and had this important reform passed in the US Senate in 2010. It aimed to monitor and control financial players on Wall Street. The reform had been wanted and pushed by Barack Obama after the subprime crisis, but the banking lobbies had fought hard to withdraw its most coercive measures. In vain. After bitter quarrels, the Wall Street ogres finally gave in. The main idea of the reform was to prevent a bankruptcy like that of Lehman Brothers and the creation of gigantic and uncontrollable banks or fund managers—such as BlackRock. To do this, regulators could impose redistricting and taxes. The reform also required these financial players to have significant and mobilized equity, to curb speculation or the securitization of credits, particularly mortgages. Financial players also had to be able to trace all of their investments and, above all, be subject to the control of a consumer financial protection office. Among these consumers, retirees, whose pensions were coveted, were particularly pampered. An article of the law was devoted to them. It limited the commission fees of management companies in the case of investment advice. It also prevented financial advisors from directing their elderly clients towards investments that risked "cutting into retirement savings." These articles were blocked and then repealed.

If the Dodd-Frank Act had continued under Trump, it is unlikely that BlackRock would have been able to grow to the proportions we know today. The reason why Donald Trump, despite his excesses and his populism, was supported by many of the most important and serious financiers of Wall Street, is due to his promise to gut Obama's banking reform. Which he did three months after his election, thanks to Steve Mnuchin, former head of Goldman Sachs, who became his Secretary of the Treasury. The Dodd-Frank Act was considered in 2010 by the press to be the most extensive reform of the

American financial system since the Great Depression of 1929. This did not move Donald Trump much, who, three months after taking office, declared: "I have asked my administration to drastically reduce Dodd-Frank because, frankly, I have so many people, friends of mine who have great businesses and they can't borrow money. They just can't get money because the banks just won't let them borrow because of the rules and regulations of Dodd-Frank."

Larry never openly criticizes Trump. He probably knows what he owes him. In an interview with Les Échos, he points out that he is a Democrat, but adds that Trump will be re-elected because "history tends to prove that when the economy remains strong, we tend to re-elect the incumbent president."

That was before the Covid crisis.

Chapter 18

Like GAFAM (Google, Apple, Facebook, Amazon, and Microsoft), Larry has built the largest and most lucrative dematerialized transnational company in thirty years. His genius consists, among other things, in making each country where BlackRock deploys its tentacles believe that it is also BlackRock's chosen land. The firm does not really have a nationality. It is Belgian in Belgium, French in France, Italian in Italy, English in London. Each time he enters a market, he sets up a business center in the capital and develops appropriate and local communication. Larry likes bakers in Paris, fries in Brussels, and pizzas in Rome.

He understood that to access this loot, the money of pensions and savers, he would have to confuse us. A fundamental question, one that cannot be ignored, then arises: in our current world, so fragile and uncertain, what political leader could decently entrust the savings or retirement of the French to American hands? And why not to the Russians or the Chinese in that case? The circle would be definitively closed.

On reflection, we are seized with fear to note that the process has begun, because no one really controls Larry Fink. And no one really controls BlackRock, except Larry and Aladdin. This is what is most distressing in this story that is being written before our eyes.

Aladdin is an artificial intelligence of the phenomenal kind. A megarobot, super-intelligent and connected to the world, who has been amassing everything he finds on the planet for thirty years.

Let's not forget Larry's obsession. His fear of taking the slightest risk. His first failure at First Boston—where he failed to predict the Fed's fall in interest rates, which caused him to lose $100 million—obsesses him. Since 1990, he has invested hundreds of millions of dollars in equipment and salaries to pay a good thousand analysts who operate six thousand computers 24/7 and process hundreds of millions of pieces of information per day. To save money, as we have seen, he has parked his computers in the middle of apple fields, in huge air-conditioned hangars on the banks of the Columbia River, where electricity is the cheapest in America. It all goes back to Wenatchee... The slightest political statement by Nadine Morano, the advice of the smallest analyst working for BFM Business, the ten-line news item in the Berry Républicain, the victory in N2 of a basketball team sponsored by Amazon, the purchase of an apartment by the sea in Oléron, of a new car at the Audi branch in the Augny commercial zone (Moselle), of a guinea pig or an Australian shepherd in a pet store in the same place, the number of firefighters intervening during a flood in Alsace, the presence of an Asian hornet nest in Charente, a death from throat cancer in Bastia, a drug seizure in Morocco, the quality of the weapons used by terrorists in Mali, the announcement of a terrible drought attacking the oaks in the Vosges forests: everything is recorded, encoded, ground up, classified, translated by Aladdin, who calculates, projects, and recalculates this data to then lay out trends and advice. In financial matters.

Should I invest in Audi? In arms sales? Sanofi's new chemo bags? Is seaside real estate profitable? Is Amazon still a good deal? Can the hard right come back to France? Will Auchan buy Truffaut pet stores? Should we invest in the manufacture of Canadair planes? In financial products privatizing the water of lakes and rivers?

Aladdin is, as we have seen, the acronym for Asset, Liability, Debt, and Derivative Investment Network. The acronym invented by Larry covers a wide range. Aladdin would therefore be an information network for investments in assets, liabilities, debts, and derivative products.

We can see Larry's idea and ambition, who invents the magical and fabulous lamp capable of fulfilling the wishes of stock market speculators and other savers: "Great Aladdin, tell me if I'm going to be rich, very rich, or just a little bit rich?"

Aladdin was created in the early 1990s by BlackRock Solutions. The goal was to develop an analysis and decision-making tool to assess bond portfolios available on the market. This risk analysis program was to ensure the company's development. Today, it is the nerve center of the BlackRock empire, which has become the largest asset management company in the world. This solution, based on the analysis and processing of collected, enriched, and constantly updated metadata, now offers internal and external users an in-depth and cross-sectional assessment of all asset classes, public or private. Aladdin is also the essential economic forecasting algorithm in the financial world. During the 2008 financial crisis, many governments close to collapse called on Larry Fink's group and its AI. These markets and contracts have allowed Larry to strengthen his grip on the global economy and present his company as a providential entity.

Between active and passive investors, we get a bit lost. BlackRock has always been an active shareholder. BlackRockers are passive investors but active shareholders. They are passive investors via their ETFs and passive funds because, for example, if the boss of Total decided to withdraw from oil to become 100% renewable, they would not be able to disinvest or resell their shares. They cannot exit and go elsewhere to see a smaller competitor that is more to their taste. They are blocked.

On the other hand, they are active shareholders because, if they cannot resell their shares, they can vote against projects they do not like in general meetings. They are all the more active shareholders because they are passive investors: it is their only lever. They are active in a very particular way. Indeed, there are forty-six of them (and they have just hired ten more people) to manage relations with about fifteen thousand companies. Not enough to interfere on a daily basis.

Until now, they were content to vote for or against the appointments (or renewals) of managers according to their interests. They are quite binary: either the managers are with them or they are against them. It is an extremely powerful lobby because a Total manager who gets fired by BlackRock is certain to never find a job in another global oil group. A BlackRock representative will soon be on the board of all the major groups and will be able to block appointments. For most of these people, getting to the board of a group is a life goal. They naturally and a priori conform to the culture of their company and the managerial strategy of the CEO.

2020 sounded the death knell for BlackRock's relative passivity, which rarely opposed the general opinion and the will of a chairman of the board of directors. They are in the process of evolving their practice by acting more and more on the fund and the strategy of the groups. With the acquisition for $1.3 billion, in March 2019, of e-Front, a French company specializing since 1999 in portfolio management and performance and risk analysis solutions, Larry scored new points and consolidated his lead over his competitors. e-Front had seven hundred clients in forty-eight countries: "We are positioned in an extremely complicated market," explains Tarek Chouman, the CEO of e-Front. "We operate in the market of private companies, whose data is not publicly available, which makes them difficult to collect... e-Front has developed its own capacity to collect data from unlisted companies. In the beginning, employees were entering this data manually into the applications, which was not really sustainable. Thanks to our growing leadership, we were able to automate this process in a way that is completely unique in the market."

This nugget of French engineering is a godsend for BlackRock, which does not hesitate to pay a billion dollars more than its English competitor Bridgepoint. Four years earlier, in March 2015, Bridgepoint had given its French founder (who was delighted to sign at this price) $300 million.

"The combination of e-Front and Aladdin, BlackRock's investment platform used by more than two hundred and twenty-five institutions worldwide, will set a new standard in investment and risk management technology," BlackRock justified in a press release.

In this sector, as we can see, information on companies' treasuries, strategies, and difficulties has inestimable value. By buying e-Front at such a high price from a European competitor, Larry is further establishing his hegemony over finance. Soon, no head will be above ground. Larry's ultimate dream.

Chapter 19

Larry may promise that our fears of seeing Aladdin make mistakes, go off the rails, or take over from humans are laughable, bullshit, and the like, but we can reasonably doubt his assurances. The literature is full of warnings, each more frightening than the last, about the dangers of overconfidence in artificial intelligence.

Elon Musk, the billionaire behind Tesla and SpaceX, has invested in an AI research program that competes with BlackRock: Google's DeepMind. He spoke to the New York Times at the end of July 2020 to express how terrified he was by the progress of Google's research. "This is a project that needs to be monitored closely because it could pose a serious threat to humanity in the very near future," Musk explains, for whom DeepMind surpasses human intelligence. "The nature of the artificial intelligence they are building crushes all humans in all areas." In this interview, Elon Musk draws a parallel between DeepMind and *Wargames*, the John Badham film released in 1983, with Matthew Broderick in the lead role. The plot is based on a computer "reputed to be more reliable than humans" being hacked by a teenage gamer. The interest of the film and its plot lies in the fact that the Wargames AI does not differentiate between the game and reality. It will thus launch a nuclear war against Russia. All the lights are red because missiles are activated by the intelligent robot. Everything could have ended badly if a human professor smarter than the others had not made it go crazy by putting it in front of a dilemma: a new game of tic-tac-toe, this game of aligning crosses, but with no other opponent than itself. The AI plays endless games and ends up winning, and losing, and getting lost. The destructive escalation is stopped just in time. The computer realizes, it's cinema, that a nuclear war, like a game of tic-tac-toe against oneself, never has a winner because the destruction is total. It speaks one last time and says in its metallic voice: "Strange game. The only winning move is not to play." With everything being digitized or almost, Musk thinks that this scenario is possible today, but that the war could go to its end. "Human intelligence will be overtaken by AI in the next five years." This does not mean that everything will be bad in five years, simply that "things will become unstable or weird," he specifies. If he decided to invest in the DeepMind program, it is to closely monitor its evolution: "People underestimate the capabilities of AI. They think it's an intelligent human, but it will go well beyond that. Very intelligent people are wrong if they think they are winning the game... We must be afraid of what we create..."

Elon Musk is criticized by many scientists for his positions considered alarmist. But four London researchers have just given credence to the billionaire's anxiety. They should worry even Larry Fink. They have in fact listed eighteen categories of potential crimes that could be committed by an AI. From the self-driving killer car to the robot warrior, they presented these cases to around thirty experts, who were asked to measure the dangerousness and imminence of these crimes. The study is the subject of a scientific article.

"The exercise resulted in a two-day workshop on 'AI and the Crime of the Future' with representatives from academia, the police, defense, government, and the private sector. The aim of the workshop was to identify and classify potential criminal and terrorist threats arising from the growing adoption and power of artificial intelligence," the protocol summarizes.

From these expert opinions, the most imminent and worrying fear by far is the development of deepfakes, these video image manipulations made by AIs that superimpose audio and video files on other videos, making scams undetectable. The most famous example is the one where Obama appears to call Trump a "dark piece of shit". The video, made by an AI, was viewed three million times in April 2018 before Obama issued a denial. It is still circulating, navigating in this murky space where truth and fiction overlap, and where it is no longer clear, unless there is investigative work, how to disentangle the true from the false.

"Convincing imitations of targets following a script can already be made, and interactive imitations could follow," note the English researchers who fear that these deepfakes will become invincible, in particular because the algorithms behind their creation are very difficult to detect.

Two dangers clearly emerge here. The first is deepfakes orchestrated by an enemy of Larry, a competitor, or a group of hackers who could artificially cause certain prices to fall, polluting Aladdin with false information. The second is the possibility of seeing Aladdin itself create undetectable deepfakes, thus rigging investment chains for the benefit of privileged individuals.

In an enlightening article on the communicators working for George Bush, whom he called the "magicians of the White House," the writer and researcher Christian Salmon mentioned "the Scheherazade strategy." It consists of telling fabulous stories to make people forget the disasters of a policy. Salmon recounts an anecdote told by Ron Suskind, Pulitzer Prize winner and journalist at the WSJ.

A few days after George Bush's election in 2002, Suskind met Karl Rove, Bush's main advisor, who mocked the journalist by saying they did not live in the same world. "You belong to what we call the reality-based community," Rove said. "You believe that solutions emerge from your judicious analysis of observable reality." Suskind nodded and muttered something about Enlightenment principles and empiricism. Rove cut him off: "That is not the way the world really works. We are an empire now," he continued, "and when we act, we create our own reality. And while you study that reality, judiciously, as you wish, we act again and create new realities, which you can study as well, and that is how things happen. We are the actors of history. [...] And you, all of you, all you have to do is study what we do."

Salmon also quotes University of Colorado professor Ira Chernus, who explains that Rove applied the "Scheherazade strategy" during Bush's two terms: "When politics sentences you to death, start telling stories—stories so fabulous, so captivating, so haunting that the king (or in this case the American people, who nominally rule our country) will forget the death sentence." Rove played on Americans' sense of insecurity, making them forget the disastrous war in Iraq by invoking collective myths of American heroism. "Karl Rove," Chernus explains, "bet that voters would be hypnotized by John Wayne stories, with 'real guys' fighting the devil on the border—enough Americans, anyway, to avoid the death sentence that voters might have pronounced against the party that led us to disaster in Iraq. [...] Rove never ceases to invent stories of good guys and bad guys for the use of Republican candidates [in Congress]. He strives to transform every election into moral theater, into a conflict pitting the moral rigor of the Republicans against the moral confusion of the Democrats. [...] Scheherazade's strategy is a big scam, built on the illusion that simple moralizing stories will give us a sense of security, regardless of what is happening in the world."

With the election of Donald Trump, the United States, along with its political, warlike, and financial machinery, seems to have turned further away from reality than under Bush and Rove. Trump and his entourage have become the producers of a fiction that they want to impose on us. BlackRock and the legend of wealth offered to the world by ETF purchases, managed by an unbeatable AI, are part of it. Larry fascinates Michel Sapin. Bruno Le Maire is lying flat on his stomach in front of him. Emmanuel Macron gives him doe-eyed looks and pats him on the shoulder. The press, especially the financial press, heaps praise on him, accusing those who criticized him during the demonstrations against pension reform of primary anti-Americanism.

This article in *Le Monde* dated January 9, 2020, provides evidence of this:

A slight air of anti-Americanism is floating over France, which owes nothing to Donald Trump. After McDonald's, the purveyor of "junk food," Amazon, the gravedigger of jobs, and Goldman Sachs, the bearer of globalized capitalism, a new giant has reawakened this sentiment, which has been firmly anchored in part of the public for two centuries: BlackRock. Only a few months ago, the world's leading asset manager was unknown to the general public; it has become the Great Satan, as it is understood to be behind the pension reform. The proof? Its founding boss, Larry Fink, sat to the right of the President of the Republic on July 10, 2019, at the Élysée Palace, during a meeting on green finance, as summarized by Julien Muguet before concluding. We cannot both regret that a significant portion of the CAC 40's 1,500 billion is in foreign hands, at the risk of seeing investments and hiring decisions made in distant headquarters, and prevent the contribution of capital necessary for the growth of companies through the retirement savings of the French. "One more effort to become capitalists!" Mr. Fink tells them. But before we turn them into a people of small shareholders... Larry can be satisfied with the storytelling achieved in such a short time. Even if he is still far behind his French asset management competitors such as Amundi, BNP Paribas, Axa, or Natixis, he can expect a lot from the elimination of special pension schemes and the desire expressed by Emmanuel Macron to see high-income executives, earning above 10,000 euros monthly, freed from social security contributions. Freed. That's liberalism, Fink-Macron version. Not quite Tocqueville's...

At the time Alexis de Tocqueville wrote *De la démocratie en Amérique*, a reference work for liberals, slavery was still the norm. A majority of liberals—Auguste Comte, Charles Dunoyer, Benjamin Constant—justified it as necessary for the development of industry and society. These same liberals dreamed of a world where enlightened power would be in the hands of an elite of engineers, scientists, and bankers. Tocqueville had curtly responded before his peers at the Academy of Sciences: "I will not admit that an unjust, immoral act, an attack on the most sacred rights of humanity, can ever be justified for a reason of utility." This moment marks a split between two currents of liberalism, whose history, presented in the media, is today too caricatured.

Utility, necessity, empty coffers, no other choice: Larry Fink and Emmanuel Macron often rely on these arguments, relayed by complacent journalists or TV hosts, to justify reforms that only the most cynical liberals would not deny. Those who dreamed and still dream of an elite of scientists and bankers to enlighten the people.

Emmanuel Macron offers the freedom for the richest to no longer finance public services. They will no longer be forced—after 120,000 euros per year—to contribute to national fraternity. Their tax rate will drop from 28% to 8%. They will thus be able to contribute their share to the financial giants. They will be able to invest their savings in high-performance and dedicated investment funds.

The money of wealthy retirees and savers has never been so close to Larry's purse. It would be madness to make pensions dependent on stock market prices, which would inevitably result from the capitalization reform desired by the BlackRock lobbyists (and François Fillon, part of the liberal right and the Enmarcheurs), who would like us to model our pension system on the American model.

The story-making and mind-formatting machine, dear to Christian Salmon, tells us a very beautiful story about pension reform. How to create a problem and a question that had no reason to exist... The pay-as-you-go pension system would be doomed in the long term, because the number of active workers would decrease.

Which is false; it is increasing. We would be facing an abysmal deficit, unable to pay our pensions despite the generosity of the first in line. The Pensions Advisory Council has shown that the deficit to finance pensions would be around 10 billion in 2025 (the range is between 7 and 17 billion). This is not huge and could be resolved without difficulty.

The pay-as-you-go pension system coupled with a point-based compensation system (which already exists in France) is viable and operational.

An interview viewed millions of times with an economics professor at Paris VIII shows in an implacable manner that there is "no problem financing pensions." This is what Gilles Raveaud explains in this video, revealing, without being denied by anyone, the existence of a reserve fund for pensions with 30 billion euros and that the supplementary pension funds have 116 billion in reserve. This is confirmed by the newspaper *Le Monde*. Emmanuel Macron had also highlighted this in his 2017 campaign, stating that there was "no problem financing pensions in France." Despite this, the propaganda continues, ever more alarmist. Social Security is said to be drained, the population is aging, young people are out of work and unwilling to finance the retirement of the elderly, public services are too expensive, salaries are overtaxed...

Fortunately, Larry Fink is there, generous and loyal. He will take good care of us.

Nonsense.

Chapter 20

In an interview with *Le Figaro*, Larry Fink discussed his approach to management and customer attraction: "I spend more time on corporate culture than on anything else. In every country where we are present, BlackRock strives to prove its raison d'être. We cannot be an American firm in France. We must be French in France, Italian in Italy, Mexican in Mexico. Many companies have forgotten that they must earn the right to operate in certain markets. Multinationals must think about this, particularly in a world where politicians are backtracking on globalization."

Question from Le Figaro: BlackRock advises central banks, such as the Greek one during the crisis. Isn't there a risk of conflict of interest with your job as an investor?

Larry's amused response, demonstrating his familiarity with the issue: "We have indeed advised states and financial institutions during the crisis—this advisory activity is also what made BlackRock profitable when it was created—and we are very proud of it. We have earned the trust of governments thanks to our ability to analyze risks. But advisory is strictly separated from asset management. We have established an iron wall between the two, and these activities are constantly audited to verify its effectiveness: everything is transparent."

Audited by whom? BlackRock is audited every three years by each of the Big Four. Since the disappearance of Arthur Andersen in 2002, the Big Five became the Big Four, then, due to their size and expansion, the Big Four have become the Fat Four: Deloitte, Ernst & Young, KPMG, and PricewaterhouseCoopers. At present, Ernst & Young is responsible for auditing the private equity giant. Essentially, for a substantial fee, these auditors produce lengthy reports that few read, issuing a stamp of approval: good for service. Larry assures us of transparency and a watertight separation between consulting and investment activities. We have to take his word for it.

Is Larry Fink's separation also impermeable? As the CEO overseeing both branches, if anyone is structurally informed about both consulting and investment activities, it is him. For instance, while advising the ECB, Larry might learn that an airline's accounts are in disarray, its shares set to plummet, and perhaps even recommend bankruptcy. At the same time, his investment branch might include this company in several ETF packages. Larry assures us that he would not use information from one channel to inform another, and that no communication occurs between branches. For the sake of his clients, Larry would thus let his salespeople sell underperforming shares rather than advising the ECB to save the company.

This example suggests a potential for corruption. Larry's challenge is to maintain this ambiguity, even if he has not yet been caught in a direct conflict of interest. He operates at the intersection of three worlds that now rely on his expertise: private banks and private equity champions, central banks and states, and stock market speculators and savers.

The concept of an "iron wall" between consulting and investment activities evokes the memory of Arthur Andersen's collapse in 2002 due to similar conflicts of interest. Arthur Andersen, once a prestigious firm known for its rigor, had a history of integrity. Founded in 1913, it grew rapidly and became a leading accountant in major American cities, expanding to Europe. For its 75th anniversary in 1988, the firm's brochure was titled "A Vision of Greatness," reflecting its growth and prominence.

However, by 2001, Arthur Andersen had 85,000 employees and generated $9 billion in revenue. Its international structure, Andersen Worldwide, had offices in 94 countries. Despite its success, concerns over conflicts of interest between its auditing and consulting branches led to scrutiny. Arthur Levitt, head of the SEC, was particularly concerned about these issues.

Arthur Andersen's close relationship with clients like Enron, which it both advised and audited, exemplified the conflict of interest. Enron's manipulation of accounts and tax avoidance, aided by Arthur Andersen, eventually led to the firm's downfall. Arthur Andersen was criticized for overlooking Enron's falsified accounts and for destroying documents during federal investigations.

Similarly, since Arthur Andersen's collapse, the Big Four have faced their own controversies. In 2014, Tesco admitted to inflating profits with PricewaterhouseCoopers' complicity. The LuxLeaks affair revealed tax avoidance schemes facilitated by PricewaterhouseCoopers. Deloitte, KPMG, and Ernst & Young have faced similar issues with other companies, showing that conflicts of interest and regulatory weaknesses persist.

The bankruptcy of Lehman Brothers, validated by Ernst & Young, further highlights the persistent issues within the auditing industry.

"Big Four: The Scandal of the Shadow Accountants," headlined *Le Monde*, which is typically cautious about criticizing international finance. From Tesco to LuxLeaks, the four major accounting firms dominating global finance are entangled in scandals and managing conflicts of interest. The journalist describes these firms as a "cartel that has become essential," auditing ninety-nine of the hundred largest British companies, the majority of those in the United States, and all the companies in the CAC 40. At 50 million euros per audit for the largest multinationals, the market is highly lucrative, allowing partners to earn an average of one million euros per year. These firms do more than audits, which constitute less than half of their revenue. They are also key players in multinational taxation, devising the most effective methods to exploit various countries' tax laws.

So, when Larry Fink faces questions about his integrity, he turns to these prestigious Fat Four. He retains their services and pays them handsomely to demonstrate the quality of BlackRock's management and the impermeability of the wall separating their advisory and investment functions.

Examining the executives of BlackRock and the Fat Four reveals concerning connections. The hierarchy at BlackRock is populated by former employees of PricewaterhouseCoopers, Ernst & Young, or KPMG. The interchangeability of personnel across these firms suggests a lack of true separation. As one might observe on LinkedIn, the same individuals often move between these companies, indicating a cozy and self-serving network.

Moreover, auditing a colossal entity like BlackRock poses significant challenges. A source familiar with the investigation into Clearstream, which also deals with vast amounts of data, explained, "Even if I had free rein, which I never do due to constant supervision, I wouldn't know where to start with such massive digital data. Imagine auditing a company generating 30,000 billion in cash." BlackRock's operations are similarly complex, making thorough auditing nearly impossible. An official from the Luxembourg Financial Sector Supervisory Commission (CSSF) confirmed that Clearstream had never been effectively audited from the outside, stating, "Clearstream and its shareholders have always self-controlled."

The situation with BlackRock is arguably even more precarious. As a firm too big to fail, it is so entrenched in the financial system that even a motivated and independent auditor would struggle to uncover irregularities amidst its vast array of accounts and transactions.

In this environment, trust is placed in the system and the machine rather than human oversight. The scenario evokes the classic science fiction image from *2001: A Space Odyssey*, where HAL, the AI-powered supercomputer, refuses to open the door for astronaut Dave Bowman, symbolizing the growing reliance on and distrust of technology and its operators.

"Open this door for me, Hal," Dave implores.

"I'm sorry, Dave, I can't do that," HAL replies.

"What do you mean by that?" asks Dave.

"This conversation is moot. Goodbye," HAL concludes.

Chapter 21

Towards the end of her book, Heike Buchter confesses that she fears the excessive influence of BlackRock "a bit like in Star Wars, when the dark side of the Force becomes too powerful," she writes. Especially since Larry Fink appears, even if he tries to mask it in most of his recent European interviews, as a staunch libertarian. "For six years, we have seen him communicate much more: on morning shows, in Washington, Madrid, London, and Berlin. He writes opinion pieces for the *Wall Street Journal*, grants interviews to the Spanish newspaper *El País* at the Ritz, speaks with the editors of *Der Spiegel*, and tells them that Germans are too afraid to invest," notes the journalist. Larry's message becomes uncomfortable for a Frenchman attached to public services, nostalgic for paid holidays and retirement at 60. According to him, citizens are too afraid of change and should take more risks to earn more. This is the essence of his message in France. Sarkozy was a proponent of similar ideas, but Larry's views are even more extreme. He is a strong supporter of extending working life: "Why should we be unproductive for a third of our lives?" he asks in his interviews. To him, "it is a blessing to work until 68," assures Heike Buchter.

Larry seems to want to offload retirement insurance onto us, forgetting that Americans, with the extension of working hours, have lost 30% of their pensions since the 2008 crisis, amid the growing dominance of private equity firms like BlackRock over the economy.

After witnessing the Belgian government's failure to reform its retirement system despite significant protests, Larry Fink is now advocating for Emmanuel Macron's government to find "the path of reason." He visits him frequently and deems our country to be on the right track, as he told *Le Monde* in September 2018: "Reforming and changing the status quo is hard, but I am convinced that the direction taken by President Macron remains the right one. BlackRock believes strongly in the future of France. Since the presidential election, we have doubled our holdings in French sovereign debt."

By examining the dates of flights of his private jet, the Gulfstream G550, to Paris and comparing them with Emmanuel Macron's schedule available on the Élysée website, we find many inconsistencies but one certainty: Larry Fink has only been coming to France since Macron's election. He visits often.

According to our calculations, the head of BlackRock has made between six and eight trips to France to meet with Emmanuel Macron, while BlackRock acknowledges only four. Before Macron's election, Larry Fink admitted to a meeting in Davos in January 2016, when Macron was François Hollande's Minister of the Economy. However, he did not confirm a meeting at the Élysée Palace in early July 2017. This meeting was apparently arranged through Jean-François Cirelli. No flights of Larry's jet are scheduled during this period. Yet, *Le Nouvel Obs* and other journalists have reported this meeting.

Larry then allegedly visited Paris on the following dates, according to his jet's flight records: — November 23, 2017, with no listed meeting; — November 9, 2018, with no official meeting; — February 4, 2019, with a gap in the Élysée schedule between 12:30 p.m. and 4:30 p.m.; — March 15, 2019, a day off at the Élysée, with nothing planned.

These flight dates do not align with the official dates provided by BlackRock and the Élysée: — A meeting in October 2017 with international investors; — In July 2019, a meeting with eight asset managers on climate (One Planet Summit), organized by Larry and his banker friends from Goldman Sachs, BNP Paribas, State Street, Natixis, Amundi, and Northern Trust.

January 20, 2020, was Choose France Day, when President Macron met with foreign investors, including Larry Fink and French business leaders.

Regardless of the confirmed trips, Larry and his team are making a concerted effort to influence France, believing that if pension reform succeeds in Paris, it will trigger a chain reaction across Europe. The attack on pension systems has become Larry's and his representative in France, the notable Jean-François Cirelli, a central focus.

Cirelli, known as Iznogoud from his time at Gaz de France, has always been involved in what can be described as controversial and self-serving maneuvers.

As a strong advocate of liberal capitalism, he has progressed from law and political science to becoming head of BlackRock France. His previous roles included advising on pension reform, working at the Treasury, and influencing the transition to the euro. As a deputy director under Prime Minister Jean-Pierre Raffarin, he played a major role in François Fillon's pension reform, which included extending contributions and initiating funded pensions.

Cirelli's career trajectory includes leading Gaz de France, which was privatized and led to significant rate increases despite promises of no privatization. He then moved to Suez, where he significantly increased his salary following the privatization. Hired by Larry Fink in 2015 as CEO of BlackRock France, Cirelli has utilized his extensive networks to advance Larry's agenda, promoting private equity and ETFs in the BlackRock style.

Cirelli's connections extend to Matignon, where he has strong ties with Alain Juppé and Édouard Philippe, who supported policies such as ending the 35-hour workweek and raising the retirement age. BlackRock's strategy in Europe involves recruiting influential figures like Cirelli and others in Berlin, London, and Greece, focusing on leveraging their political and economic influence to advance its financial products and agendas.

Emmanuel Macron's special advisor, Philippe Grangeon (former CFDT communications director, interim president of LREM in 2018, advisor to Nicole Notat), is trying in particular to maintain dialogue between Emmanuel Macron and Laurent Berger, the current leader of the CFDT union, despite his opposition to any cost-cutting measures being largely ignored. At Matignon, Benoît Ribadeau-Dumas, for his part, defends fiscal positions aimed at financially balancing the system. However, this tension does not extend to the interest shown in asset managers in general and BlackRock in particular. Both heads of the executive welcome them with the same benevolence and open the doors of the Republic's salons wide to them," she concludes. Curtain. BlackRock is the arm that aims to undermine all projects of emancipation and nationalization, wherever initiatives not aligned with BlackRock are taken. Where BlackRockers intervene, the welfare state has no place.

As I wrote on my canvases eight years ago, Larry Fink has mastered the art of ignoring the poor and making them even poorer. Of course, he never puts it that way. Larry is adept at bouncing back and making us believe in his good fortune, as seen in this interview published in Le Figaro, where he emphasized rigor and benevolence towards his clients:

"You are one of the most powerful men on the planet. What responsibility do you bear?" the French reporter asks.

What a thrill to hear a journalist affirm that you are at the top of the Power and Money planet after an interview with the man who took the Élysée and wants to put France and its elderly back to work! Cross your legs, adjust your gold-rimmed glasses. Think about how far you have come since your early days at First Boston. Think about Lorri and tomorrow's pancakes. About the North Salem weather vanes that spin faster than the brain of the person in front of you. Finally, tell yourself that you deserve your billions. Smile with modesty and condescension at the same time. And deliver a weighty answer, if possible:

"My responsibility has not changed in the last thirty years, and I think about it every day," Larry recites. "We are responsible for the savings of millions of people around the world, more than any other institution, and our job is to make sure that their financial future is the best possible."

What altruism! What selflessness! Larry assures us that he reminds his employees every day:

"The important thing is not the amounts we handle, but the savings of each teacher, each police officer, each soldier that we manage. We must earn the trust of our customers every day, by doing the best we can in terms of performance, but also by explaining to them the importance of the long term."

Come on! We would almost shed a tear. Holy Larry! Why stop there...

"In this regard, we are not efficient enough. Too many people remain focused on the short term. Too many French people keep their savings in their checking accounts, and that is not a good strategy!"

That's for sure. It is better to leave your savings to Jean-François Cirelli and BlackRock. Stop worrying about it and trust them...

The gamble was thrown.

Chapter 22

In 2019, BlackRock collected more than a billion dollars per day. The fund manager saw its assets under management swell by approximately $429 billion, marking a record increase of almost 25%. The assets managed by the American giant are approaching $7,500 billion.

Behind the technology, as Bernard Stiegler tells us, lies an ideology: that of the all-powerful financial markets, of which BlackRock is the latest avatar. Behind Aladdin's algorithm, a vision emerges—a world without surprises where the law of the strongest and best-prepared always prevails. This vision is a heresy; it leaves no room for humanity or the social body. Behind BlackRock's ultra-high-performance equipment and processes are mathematicians, analysts, computer scientists, physicists, and cyberneticians who design them. They are paid to avoid bugs and revolts. Their way of imagining society, their perception of life itself, coincides with the interests of those who feed them and use them.

Fucking Larry.

BlackRock, it's his good looks, his confidence. This way he has of flaunting his power. Long live capitalism. Long live the great washing machine that turns, washes us, and regenerates the economic fabric. Long live Aladdin and his advice for tomorrow.

Larry Fink depresses me.

I'm at a standstill. As I progress through this story, I discover whole sections of information, connections, and declarations that I had not imagined, confirming my initial intuition. BlackRock's growing share overflows into the financial markets. It impacts our lives. It is dangerous.

I am writing to a friend who worked in this environment and is now retired. He nicknamed the boss of BlackRock "Larry the Embrouille."

Dialogue: — Tell me... I'm still on BlackRock. I've lined up fifteen chapters. I'm rereading myself, particularly this excerpt concerning ETFs, sold by Fink to millions of stock market speculators. On reflection, we're hit because no one controls the mess... — I confirm... So what? No one controls anything. In France, you've been thinking a lot about Kerviel. But there are Kerviels everywhere. Every bank and investment fund is a time bomb... — If BlackRock's clients unilaterally decided to withdraw their stakes, the stocks of companies all over the world where the firm has invested would plummet almost instantly. No one would be able to buy back the ETFs. — For them to get to that point, there would have to be a major event. The guys who buy ETFs do it over the phone. If you want to sell, you have to call and justify it. It takes time... — OK, but what would happen? A collapse? A crash? Or not much? Do you have any ideas? — Well, no. ETFs are special. You buy shares in a fund that reflects a category, often broad and global. The main risk is that the category goes belly up or the global system crashes. The latter is theoretically possible but practically unlikely. It would take something huge. Especially since today, the reality is that half of the financial markets are held by central banks. They've bought everything and invented money... That's why BlackRock and Larry are constantly courting them. The problem is that they depend on BlackRock as much as BlackRock depends on them. — Let's take the CAC 40 ETFs... BlackRock owns more than 5% of about twenty companies... If the CAC ETF collapses, what happens? — Nothing... Otherwise, the markets would have crashed since March 2019. They are holding steady. Central banks are maintaining prices. It's not the ETF that's falling. It's the companies first; then the ETF if it's poorly weighted. — And what's the effect on reality? — The principle of the ETF is to spread the risks, to dilute. BlackRock has this status today because it owns many ETFs, each having a small piece of a big company. — So, the collapse is pretty unlikely? — For a collapse, it would take either a rapid global meltdown or rotten management of one or more ETFs. But for BlackRock, it doesn't change much. They took their commissions... — On the bond market and stocks, BlackRock steals clients from the banks, right? Especially if Aladdin becomes operational? — Yes, and this hegemonic position is starting to annoy. The risk for BlackRock would be a coalition of banks or a Kerviel-type operation. That a person plays the store's money while forgetting that it's not his. That could cause significant damage. BlackRock does not own 1/10,000 of the sums managed... I continue: — Another question I ask myself... I can see the game of the ECB and the central banks, or the Fed... the printing presses that bail out... But what is the risk? The story can go on forever... Aladdin is going to become the Google of the markets, supposed to predict risk in real time?! So, if there is a big mistake or a flaw, Aladdin must see it? — Not necessarily. The predictive aspect of Aladdin is Larry Fink's advert. Aladdin cannot predict anything; it just allows you to find a reason after the fact if things go wrong. — So, if Aladdin is in trouble, BlackRock could be swept away... — It could. — The structure set up by Larry is essentially based on promises. It all comes down to Ponzi schemes, really? — Yes, and one day, if to end the year 300 million results are missing and his store sees its share price fall, then he will try to cover it up. I'm confusing you. I take, say, 300 million out of 30 billion in a week... — But where does he take them from? — They are discreetly taken from his clients who think they are safe with cool ETFs invested in water or wind turbines... No luck, the next day, Kim launches a nuclear missile while shouting. The market is down 15% in three days. And Larry takes a 5 billion loss. The company is in trouble. And his clients are screwed. From there, they sell like crazy. But if there are no more buyers, it's a disaster! — Could something like that happen? — Yes, of course. BlackRock invests 10 billion in equity in Mexican oil projects, for example. Slim's son is on the board, which helps... But if things go badly and we find out that the 10 billion were not quite for the clients... — In a case like that, the company will hide it... — Yes. The company still announces 5 billion in profits per year on 12 in turnover... Sixteen thousand employees... There is a huge amount of cash stagnating at BlackRock. It's tempting to use it as long as its clients don't sell. Seven thousand billion in investments, a third of which are ETFs. Five billion in profits on 12, that's huge...

Since I took on the challenge of writing about BlackRock, I have spent hours on the Internet tracking down the slightest bit of information, trying to cross-check my sources. I've mostly read the blogs and newsletters of various financial analysts. It is a hyper-competitive sector dominated by charlatans. Well before the Internet, analysts were already in competition, and predictive models, more or less amusing, vied with each other in ingenuity. Nowadays, the "golden" number has been abandoned, but technical analysts or "chartists"—those who assure you that their calculations are correct by tinkering with sticks and candles—flood the stock market sites. Predicting crashes has always been part of the game and the Holy Grail. I remember a Belgian analyst from Banque Bruxelles Lambert who predicted a stock market crash every year to his management. He was eventually proven right over the years, and those who didn't know his quirky methods took him for a great soothsayer.

While rummaging around, I had two notable encounters. One with a young French financial analyst based in Lausanne. The other with the American guru of crash prediction. Both have insights into BlackRock that reinforce my belief that my intuition regarding the dangerousness of Larry's firm was correct. And that I was right, after the censorship of my preface, to undertake what seems like a hazardous journey.

Guy de la Fortelle is not a soothsayer and does not manage portfolios but regularly delivers analyses on the Internet. Why not take them into account? The financial bigwigs hailed Bernard Madoff very low, the day before his fall. Guy de la Fortelle has not fallen; he does not claim to establish a new financial religion; he only offers his opinions on his website.

In a video posted in January 2020 on his blog, he compares ETFs to laundry detergent and BlackRock to a supermarket that rigs the market by flooding it with discount products...

BlackRock wants to become the Google of investment. It is the last possible growth relay for the monster that already manages $21,000 billion, directly or indirectly: as much as the GDP of the United States and more than the entire Nasdaq, which includes the American tech giants: Google, Microsoft, Apple, Amazon... We are now well aware of all the problems posed by Google's hegemony. They are nothing compared to the delusion of power of BlackRock and its founder Larry Fink, who, at almost seventy years old, still has time to execute his plan but not a minute to lose. Like Jules Verne's monster, few people can distinguish the cogs of the Nautilus behind the mysterious and fantastical beast. Here, the 0s and 1s of the algorithmic monster have replaced the sheet metal and gears... We have changed millennia. Captain Nemo is called Larry

Fink, more amiable but no less obscure than the antihero of *Twenty Thousand Leagues Under the Sea*. And like Captain Nemo, Fink seems indifferent to the welfare of the people around him and solely devoted to a vision of the world where he alone rules.

All in all, BlackRock is the caprice of our age: an autonomous entity, whose top manager does not address the public, concerned only with maximizing the already exorbitant financial power of the American fund and his private fortune. He is the most powerful man in the world, with only one goal: to control everything, endlessly. As the title of Larry Fink's 2018 letter said: "A New World Order"...

What will happen in the long run? The algorithmic monster of BlackRock will devour the financial markets. Larry Fink, like the characters of the great writers of science fiction, follows the same path. In a world where the winner always wins, BlackRock's power, despite its enormous wealth, will inevitably face failures. An algorithm, no matter how powerful, will never master the real world completely.

Chapter 23

Michael Burry's argument is based on the amount of ETF trading in the S&P 500. For about a year, more ETFs have been traded than actual company shares, leading to potential distortions in the index. According to Burry, this overreliance on ETFs, which are speculative bets rather than actual shares, could destabilize the market because the index no longer reflects the true market reality. This is a complex issue, even for experienced traders.

To illustrate this, consider two private schools with students of varying levels in their second year of high school. An inspector must grade them. In one school, teachers and school life proceed normally. In the other, students with an average of at least ten out of twenty are guaranteed to graduate with at least that average. Each year, you calculate the general average of both schools. Which school's overall grade would be the fairest? This is similar to Burry's question: what is the value of an index where a majority of the stocks are held by automated funds that disregard the actual economy and market realities?

As I write this, I think of the novice who sees the stock market as a curious entity with little impact on our lives. Let's use a metaphor: imagine a crowded cinema where stock owners and ETF owners mix and try to exit. Each day, Spy ETFs are traded five times more than Coty shares, the French makeup company, which is the smallest in the S&P 500. Similarly, the Gap clothing brand and Xerox photocopiers are traded much less frequently than Spy ETFs, and for Ralph Lauren, the ratio is even more extreme. This discrepancy could signal a future catastrophe.

Let's consider the role of buyers and sellers of these ETFs. Big banks and financial institutions, to avoid market imbalances, buy or sell shares of the ETF to balance differences. However, during a crisis, if everyone sells at once, these market makers will need to sell the stocks comprising the ETF, including less liquid small caps like Ralph Lauren, which have much lower trading volumes. It's like arriving with seventy crates of tomatoes to sell in a market with only one crate and a line of buyers, or at the exit of a crowded cinema with a very small door. If someone shouts that those who don't leave immediately will lose all their money, panic will ensue.

Burry asserts, supported by graphs, research, and statistics, that in a crisis, there will be far fewer buyers than there are shares to sell to balance the ETFs, unless companies buy their own shares, further distorting the market. For instance, the price of Apple shares, the highest on the market, is inflated by Apple's own share buybacks. Market makers, primarily big banks, risk not finding buyers for these shares, leading to inevitable price drops and a vicious circle. In March 2020, the declines observed in the market were halted by the Federal Reserve's rapid intervention. The question is whether the Fed will be able to respond as effectively in the next crisis.

In France, where ETFs and passive management currently pose less risk on the CAC 40, the situation is different. However, with Larry Fink and his associates making their presence felt in Europe, France is not immune to these concerns.

Burry predicts that the next crisis will be a severe liquidity and credit issue, similar to the one that burst the real estate bubble in 2008. Back then, many believed the real estate market was invincible, and Burry was dismissed as a prophet of doom. Today, his warnings about ETFs are met with less skepticism, though his article on Bloomberg did not provoke significant market reactions. His warnings, issued in September 2019, seem to have been largely ignored until now. For example, if the market collapses, shares of smaller companies like Coty will fall faster within ETFs, causing market makers to sell stocks quickly in a market with limited buyers, exacerbating the downturn. The metaphor of the cinema exit illustrates how panic can cause massive sell-offs.

Guy de la Fortelle confirms that the market's stability in March 2020 was due to central banks' intervention. This situation is not solely the fault of ETFs, but they contribute to market distortions by weakening smaller, less liquid stocks. Criticizing Burry for his concerns because ETFs weathered the March crisis overlooks the fact that central banks intervened heavily to support ETFs.

Central banks and large asset managers like BlackRock are advancing in solidarity, creating a vicious cycle. This is what Burry criticizes, and it was also sensed by John Bogle, founder of Vanguard, who passed away in January 2019. Bogle, a respected figure in finance, was wary of ETFs and believed they encouraged speculation, undermining the market's response to supply and demand. He warned that if ETFs surpassed 50% of the US stock market, the "big three" (BlackRock, Vanguard, and State Street) would control 30% of the market, which he thought would not serve the national interest.

While some view ETFs as a great investment due to their simplicity and low fees, others, like Bogle and Burry, see them as a risk. Critics argue that central banks supporting ETFs with interventions could lead to dangerous consequences if such support ceases.

With BlackRock leading the ETF market, both the CAC 40 and S&P 500 indices appear distorted. Burry's warnings seem plausible, and if central banks and asset managers continue their current strategies, market ratings may become disconnected from the actual quality of companies. The critical question is: until when will this continue? As long as ETFs are thriving, many seem unconcerned, but when the market crashes, Burry's predictions may prove accurate.

Chapter 24

As I write these lines and try to finish this book before it finishes me, I discover an article from the *Financial Times* that I had archived and that a Swiss newspaper curiously resurfaced a month later. The *FT* journalist had the good idea of taking an interest in ETFs and of bringing the debate to a place where it was not expected.

On the interest of observing ETFs to prevent crises... We are getting a bit hard here. Those who yawn can move on to the next chapter. At the same time, it is full of birdsong. Do you know many *FT* pen-pushers who write poetry?

Under the title "ETFs are the canary in the bond coal mine," the journalist explains that ETFs must be observed very closely because, like the canary that dies warning the miner of the firedamp explosion, they are the harbinger – and ultimately morbid for them – of the next crash. The point is not so far removed, even if the angle and target are different, from that of Michael Burry. Should we recall that it was not the song of the canary that warned of the firedamp explosion, but the cessation of the song due to the gases responsible for the explosion? The *Financial Times* looks back at the financial crash narrowly avoided at the time of the COVID crisis in March 2020 and tries to measure its scope and the internal regulatory mechanisms. If we are to believe the newspaper adored by financiers, pension funds, and large managers of our savings invested heavily in ETFs after the COVID crisis, which saw countries' economies slow down and close behind national borders. These stock market investments generated interesting returns for managers like BlackRock, providers of ETFs, and made asset managers more solid in a priori stable investments. But it also embarrassed them because usual transactions declined significantly. The markets lacked liquidity. Yet they had to be kept afloat. So banks and institutions bought and sold stocks and bonds in a somewhat forced, artificial way. The *FT* notes that in early March 2020, the price of ETFs "collapsed so dramatically that the funds lost their link to the prices of the underlying corporate bonds. Some were trading at a 5% discount" to their value. At the time of this breakdown, no one could explain it, so sudden and significant was the fall. Here comes the revelation of the *FT* article: the fluctuations in ETF prices preceded the fall in prices: "This volatility did not occur because trading dried up; on the contrary, daily trading volumes in ETFs exploded, increasing by 250% compared to before the crisis, and investor redemptions were very modest in March compared to other asset classes. So it seems that investors responded to the corporate bond market freeze by using ETFs to hedge risks, research prices, and remove exposures they didn't like. ETFs were a crutch for investors..."

The fact that there was no redemption is a bad signal. The banks had no one to resell the shares to. This is the famous liquidity problem that could have caused the crash if the Fed had not compensated.

Market players – traders, analysts, bankers, stock market speculators – then get scared and say to themselves: "Shit, COVID is going to blow everything up, I have to sell my shares quickly to buy something more stable and diversified, an index, an ETF..." And boom, there's a rush... Are you following me?

According to the *Financial Times*, if the Fed had not stepped in late March to buy corporate bonds and ETFs en masse, the market could have collapsed, leading to stock markets falling and banks, companies, and institutions failing. The article concludes that while banks played a major role in the 2008 financial crisis, ETFs "matter much more now, and not just in the world of corporate bonds."

How should we interpret this attention paid to ETFs? With this new index, we are indeed faced with the weak link in the financial markets. The one that will give way first in the event of a problem. The image of the dying canary takes on its full meaning here. In the event of another firedamp storm on the markets, ETF owners will once again be on the front line. The Fed saved them in March, but will the operation be able to be repeated, or will ETFs be the first to be sacrificed?

Banks and private equity firms like BlackRock are playing it safe. They provide the liquidity for ETFs and make profits when everything is going well, but they do not take risks since they do not hold these ETFs themselves. They work for their clients. Private or central banks need crises to generate volume and commissions. They are paid on volume. An ETF does not need a crisis; it buys and sells constantly to balance its basket of values. Its compensation will not increase with the crisis...

What the *FT* article does not say, but which makes the situation even more murky, is that these massive purchases of bonds and ETFs, and therefore the rescue of the American economy by the Fed, were made possible thanks to BlackRock, as the press explained at the time. "When the Fed calls on BlackRock for its asset purchases," was the headline in *Les Échos* on March 25, 2020: "When times are tough, central banks turn to BlackRock. The Federal Reserve announced Tuesday that it had called on the company to take charge of several of its new asset purchase programs. [...] A new mark of the influence of the world's largest manager," writes the newspaper, which specifies that BlackRock will notably pilot "two vehicles that will buy corporate debt on the primary and secondary markets, each with $10 billion in capital provided by the Fed. Like the ECB's asset purchases, the bonds in question will have to be of good quality, therefore issued by companies that are relatively sound from a financial point of view." And there, a very red light comes on and the conflict of interest is obvious, because "solid companies issuing good quality bonds" are not many on the market. BlackRock is certainly at the forefront. The firm, commissioned by the Fed, will therefore choose to buy products in a market where it is itself a leader.

Seeing the criticism coming, Larry was quick to communicate that his Financial Markets Advisory division, in charge of these programs, was "strictly separated from its other activities... precisely in order to prevent any conflict of interest." And Larry specified that he trusts his "Aladdin platform to monitor these portfolios." Like: "It's an AI, it's autonomous, it'll choose the best in the bunch, if it falls on us, it's because we're the best..."

Well, let's see.

With Larry, no problem. No one, neither at the Fed, nor in the banks, nor at the *FT*, nor at *Les Échos*, found fault with this argument. It went down like a letter in the post.

It's the story of a large vegetable garden divided into plots managed by a former banker. Each plot has a farmer at its head. One of them decides to stuff his vegetables and fruits with GMOs to resist the rain, the cold, the heat, the insects. The vegetable garden lives off its own sales on the surrounding markets. Birds never visit his plot, but he doesn't care. His yield and growth are optimal. Everything is going well until a first invasion of insects. Only the vegetables of the GMO farmer resist. The banker takes advice from him and asks him to help the other farmers by giving them some doping products. The guy does it and it works. With the money raised, he doesn't buy other vegetable gardens but sells doping products to his neighbors. Then comes global warming and drought. His vegetables, which all have the same bland flavor, are the only ones growing. Yet everyone wants them. The farmers are forced to line up, and the plots are full of these fruits and vegetables inflated with GMOs. The banker breathes. Thanks to the GMO farmer, his vegetable garden is saved.

Here we are, with Larry and his hormone-pumped ETFs, and the Fed boss as a banker managing a vegetable garden. It's a bit of a soft version of the story that billionaire Carl Icahn told on the TV show, assuring us that Larry, accompanied by the Fed boss, were going to throw us into the bottom of the ravine by driving a bus sideways without brakes. My metaphor may seem less radical than Icahn's, but I would like to continue it. Some of the farmers' customers will inevitably realize the poor quality of the vegetables and the lack of flavor and diversity in their products. Some farmers will start less intensive crops but more adapted to the situation. Microcrops that will gradually nibble away at and reinvigorate the vegetable garden and the market. The birds will come back to sing in these plots. Smart, rich, and informed as he is, but above all worried about seeing his sales drop, Larry will inevitably go and breathe their air and sweet-talk these new farmers, pockets full of money: "So, how much do you sell your tomatoes for? And your vegetable garden?"

In finance as in agriculture, the question is whether everything can be bought... Larry thinks so.

Chapter 25

BlackRock is a protean monster, crisscrossed by a thousand currents, throwing its tentacles all over the planet, feeding on the work of men. Its brain is an AI called Aladdin. Its pilot is an old cowboy whose affable exterior hides the anxiety of doing wrong. The slightest mistake would be paid for in cash. The engine and fuel – the blood – of this monster is our money. It takes it from us, invests it, makes margins, and returns it to us with, if possible, a slight capital gain. To survive, BlackRock must develop and pump us again and again. That is its reason for being. Larry's job is to make us forget this.

BlackRock's primary capital is its image, its reputation, its corporate identity. What I have in mind is still confusing. I want to address the issue of central banks. We will understand nothing of BlackRock's influence if we do not integrate this giant into the banking system—and its dysfunctions. I know, the subject is boring, but hey. One more effort. I have a few more bullets to fire...

Given the state of the financial markets, central banks on life support, and the finances of states drained, BlackRock wants to invest the money from our European and French retirements in its circuits at the worst possible time. If we compare the evolution of the CAC 40 to that of French growth since 1988, we can see without fail that in the long term, the CAC is always above French growth. This means that companies capture more wealth than they create for the country. They inevitably take this wealth from employees and retirees.

Investing in the stock market in the hope of long-term gains is based on the hope that capital will continue to capture more and more wealth from salaries and pensions. This amounts to sawing off the branch on which an employee or retiree is sitting. Logical, right?

BlackRock and the banks are pushing governments to promote savings in life insurance and direct part of retirement contributions to the financial markets. But the markets have become very unstable. They are our dinosaurs. The stage after "too big to fail" is "too big to survive." The markets have become enormous, vaporous, and distant from the real economy. In the United States, companies are often forced to redistribute more than 100% of their profits to their shareholders. This prevents the investment, innovation, and wage growth that a healthy economy needs. France is following the same path. The markets are destroying the economy by promising ever more economic growth. The contradiction has become irreconcilable.

"For me, it's as if BlackRock wanted to put its hand in the honey pot. Except that it is already empty, and once we put it in, not only will we realize the deception, but who, do you think, will be accused of having emptied it?" asks analyst Guy de la Fortelle.

In its original businesses, BlackRock has filled up. Its position, often close to 40% of volumes, is approaching that of a monopoly. Especially since its main competitor and largest shareholder, Vanguard, also holds significant weight.

The prospect, if Larry continues to develop his investment branch, is to be confronted with antitrust laws, which are very coercive in the USA. Added to this is a risk of increased competition due to BlackRock's phenomenal success. And competition that is becoming exhausting, since BlackRock works with commissions of between 0.1% and 1%. This is the risk of all high-volume businesses, whose procedures are automated.

Larry will have to change his model if he wants to continue to make profits. He started with Mexican oil and his alliance with Carlos Slim around Pemex. Larry invests in oil, pipelines, refineries. He also invests, or at least announces that he does, in green energy. We have heard his growing interest in investments labeled "climate change." It is about changing the playing field by minimizing risks. Always the same obsession.

Larry seems to want to invest in heavy, sovereign infrastructure concessions involving countries and politics: oil, gas, energy, construction of dams, highways, high-speed trains, nuclear power plants, port areas, reconstruction of a country after a tragedy...

Given its size, BlackRock's investments quickly become disproportionate: nothing under a billion, but it can quickly climb to 10, 50, or even 100 billion.

This seems logical when you have 7,500 billion in assets. To make these investments, Larry must think, consult, negotiate, weigh, and have a clear strategic vision. The right to make mistakes is not allowed, unless you want to drag economies and countries down with you. This type of project easily goes off the rails if not controlled. Let us remember the collapse of Eurotunnel shares. We start with a quote of 5 billion, and we quickly arrive at 30. And the EPRs. And the dams in the Amazon...

The right to make mistakes is not allowed because if the investments – in the long term – are not profitable, the losses become stratospheric.

BlackRock's core business was until now to ensure a regular return to its clients, who paid their pensions every month. It is a clockwork mechanism. In this context, BlackRock can lose, but not too much and especially not for long.

For such heavy investments, you have to be able to absorb significant losses over long periods without flinching. When, at a smaller level, Vincent Bolloré invests in electric batteries, he can withstand fifteen years of deficits before making money.

Rumors in the financial press suggest that BlackRock might drop investments in armaments or coal (not oil yet) to move towards ecology and the fight against global warming. But what if a war breaks out with Iran? BlackRock loses on both fronts: armaments take off again, and ecology plummets.

This shows the importance of these strategic choices. Often, in multinationals, boards of directors weigh and re-weigh decisions. At BlackRock, SuperLarry is at the controls. He is both Hulk and Magneto—muscles and big arms that unleash fire, and a brain that constantly calculates. Everything goes through him. Is he competent to choose an XXL market? Not sure. We have seen him lose crazy amounts of money in real estate. This is not at all reassuring.

The losses could, in the event of an unexpected geopolitical earthquake, be abysmal and wipe out BlackRock, which has little equity.

Larry Fink built BlackRock on a mechanism that leaves little room for doubt and creativity. In this respect, Aladdin does not have—contrary to the group's communication—long-term prospective qualities. These have never been demonstrated, in any case.

Larry and his development department are looking for spaces to occupy, infrastructures to buy in emerging or post-emerging countries that are not too unstable—Mexico, India, Pakistan, Turkey, etc. He no longer has much choice. Inaction would kill him.

France, since Emmanuel Macron came to power, is a good lead. Not only to capture pensions. Covid has put privatization projects like ADP on hold, but others are under consideration. We saw it with the disastrous privatization of highways: a liberal country is capable of selling everything to bring in foreign currency and feed its golden boys.

A rumor has been circulating that France is going to sell several of its dams, or about 10% of the country's electricity. A seemingly safe and quiet return, except that two dams are in poor condition. It would therefore be necessary to sell a group of dams. This type of project aligns with the perspective of a government of enmarcheurs. A leak from the Elysée informed us that this question had been raised during discreet conversations between Larry, Jean-François Cirelli, his right-hand man in France, and Emmanuel Macron's entourage.

Let's imagine a serious problem in these privatized dams, an earthquake, a collapse. What will BlackRock do? And the State? We are in the case of Fukushima or, closer to us, that of the collapsed bridge in Genoa.

Larry is on the lookout, his checkbook at hand. He has already doubled his investments in France. He is the biggest shareholder of the CAC 40. He is nervous. "Hey, Manu, how much are you selling me your damn dams?"

Chapter 26

In ten years of ultra-rapid expansion, BlackRock has become the manager of a significant portion of the savings of the US population. Pushed and guided by Larry Fink, boosted by Aladdin and ETF trading, the firm is attacking the planet with jet travel, mechanical smiles, tailored communication, promises, and thinly veiled threats against those who oppose it. BlackRock hires local politicians and senior civil servants to achieve its ends.

It knows where the gold is that guarantees the creation of money, and France has no shortage of it. We are the fourth-largest reservoir on the planet, even if the level drops. The central banks of countries and the ECB have the mission of creating and regulating money. We say "to print money" or "to mint money," as in the Middle Ages. Nations are built on their currency.

After the war, central banks held a solid, regal, and important status. They were the pillars of nations. Before, it was reinforced concrete. It was the State. It was de Gaulle, Mitterrand, or Clemenceau. Today, it is Macron, Hollande, and Sarkozy—a moment of relaxation. Nicolas Sarkozy sold 20% of our gold in 2004. A bad choice. But hey, we have the elected officials we deserve.

So, the central banks. They must repay the debts of countries and take the best care of the savings of the populations. In the United States, Larry, because of the links that have become endemic between the Fed and BlackRock, has an open table at the Treasury. The examples of the transition from private to public in the USA are legion.

The most notable recruitment at BlackRock was that of former Fed Vice Chairman Stanley Fischer in February 2019. A year after leaving his position as number two at the Federal Reserve, the old banker (75 years old), conservative and reactionary, joined BlackRock to become a senior advisor to the BlackRock Research Institute. "His experience and expertise will help our investors and clients understand the impact of global developments on their portfolios," Larry said happily at the time of his appointment.

BlackRock and the Fed: it's a rock and a hard place.

"This is not the first time that a central banker has joined a private financial institution," reports *Les Échos*, citing the case of Ben Bernanke, who, after chairing the Fed, was hired by the giant Pimco (for Pacific Investment Management Company, the bond fund owned since 2000 by the German insurer Allianz).

In Europe, the trend is the same. In 2015, the year Bernanke was hired, Pimco also hired former British Prime Minister Gordon Brown and Jean-Claude Trichet, former governor of the Bank of France and president of the ECB. The same one who has always been very cool about opening up European markets to American funds. Let's not forget that Philipp Hildebrand, former head of the Swiss National Bank, fired because of an insider trading affair, is vice-president of BlackRock, specifically responsible for the development (I almost wrote invasion) of BlackRock in Europe. The priority issue for BlackRock is to reach the savings and pensions of Europeans, after having put those of American workers in its pocket.

In the final analysis, it is the money earned by the work of the populations that guarantees the solidity of a country's currency and the value of its debt.

BlackRock will never go to Africa...

As for central banks, the situation has worsened with the Covid crisis.

The holders of financial power remain the major American banks (let's never forget that the Fed belongs to them). They control the global credit market via the dollar. Central banks are no longer masters of the game. They give the impression of chasing events and living at the expense of BlackRock and its ilk. If Ben Bernanke or Alan Greenspan, at the Fed, or even Mario Draghi, when he was at the head of the ECB, could create an illusion and resist a little, how can we imagine that Christine Lagarde, now at the head of the ECB, or Jerome Powell, the insipid lawyer appointed by Trump to the Fed, could oppose the dictates of American funds and be the real order-givers?

Beyond BlackRock, the future and strategies of central banks is a subject of concern largely ignored by the media.

I know, it's complicated. I have been bumping into this wall and these questions since I started this job. I may be wrong, or I may seem like a crank, but since I have been navigating these murky waters of finance, I have the feeling that few people are aware of what is going on. Not a conspiracy or a crash, just an improbable drift, of which BlackRock is the latest catastrophic symbol. And Larry Fink the evil figure. The Magneto of the X-Men...

Let's take France and Europe. The euro is a common currency, not a single one. Each country is responsible for its euros and their exchanges. Target is responsible for compensating. Germany still has a clearly positive balance; Italy and Spain are lagging behind; France is navigating blindly...

To finance its public policies or the Covid crisis, a state borrows mainly in the form of bonds. The interest rates on these loans depend on the rating given by the rating agencies. The central banks in the eurozone are integrated into the ECB and have been able to call on the ESM (European Stability Mechanism) since 2012. Monetary sovereignty, due to the European treaties, has therefore disappeared. No government can act as it wishes, even with the massive support of its population: its economy is decided in Brussels and Frankfurt.

What we saw happen in 2008, and even more blatantly in 2020, with the Covid crisis, shows a historic change in the financing conditions of states. Before the banking crisis of 2008, the markets were open, and the central banks played the role of local actors and moderators. This meant that if an actor, even on a national scale, made a mistake, he could have the entire planet against him. This is what happened in 1992 when the billionaire George Soros speculated against the Bank of England.

The system is almost 100% integrated; everything is regulated by a handful of central banks. They are interconnected and do, more or less, what they want. This is a new situation that few people are aware of. Today, the ECB, the Fed, the Bank of France, the Bank of Japan, the Bank of England, the Swiss National Bank, and the other national banks communicate daily and regulate everything above the states, within the BIS, the Bank for International Settlements. Its characteristics allow it to function as a micro-state, a principality escaping the usual legal regime of any national financial institution...

Everyone, starting with the little people, is stuck in and by this system.

And BlackRock in this maelstrom? Larry has spies everywhere, who advise on debt or credit buybacks and count the points. France has become a privileged hunting ground. In this behind-the-scenes game, of which we are rarely informed, the Banque de France (under the aegis of the ECB) does not play collectively, but speculatively, as the economist and founder of Attac, Dominique Plihon, explains to the Bastamag website: "The challenge is to renationalize the debt, as in Japan, where most of the debt is held by its nationals. Conversely, in France, our debt is held for more than half by international investors, such as BlackRock, who make it an object of speculation. What matters is to reduce the power of finance over states. This is why we do not want to issue securities that, tomorrow, would give financiers the weapons to impose austerity policies, particularly in Europe." In principle, a treaty in Europe prohibits states from running a deficit of more than 3%: this is the fundamental law of the EU. In practice, everyone does as they please. Everything is negotiated, but between themselves, between decent people. What can an economic system mean whose fundamental law, applicable to all, is in reality constantly renegotiated by a few, in the back rooms of the EU? If there are no more rules at the top of the system, why should they be imperative at the bottom? Central banks, including the ECB, are prohibited from buying government debt, which only markets must buy. This rule makes it possible to spread the risks attached to these debts over a very large area, from one end of the planet to the other. In practice, through selected private banks—what are called SVTs, Treasury Securities Specialists—the ECB buys up all government debts. Which is forbidden. But the ECB shirks the responsibility by explaining that it buys up these debts from the selected banks, which, in the process, gorge themselves.

Gorged themselves.

Gorged themselves too much.

I warned you. I'm in trouble.

I even have to reread myself to understand what I'm writing...

The ECB never says that these buybacks from banks take place barely thirty seconds after the latter have bought the debts from the states, and passed it all on by taking their margins on gigantic volumes of debt. Nor that BlackRock, which is not a bank, benefits from them... The result of the operations: we allow ourselves to do anything, anyhow, we just have to agree among ourselves. And public debts explode. But what is public debt? Ultimately, deferred tax, which taxpayers will simply have to pay later.

Or not.

Chapter 27

Between Paris, Berlin, Madrid, Rome, and Frankfurt, a few hundred people are gambling with our future without informing us or warning us about who they are and what they do. Smile... when the bill comes, the same people will come and explain that it is up to us to pay it.

Eighteen banks have been accredited or "co-opted" by the Fed, the ECB, and the central banks to buy our public debts. In other words, they were self-selected. Five American banks (Citigroup, Bank of America, Merrill Lynch, Morgan Stanley, JPMorgan Chase, Goldman Sachs), four French (BNP Paribas, Société Générale, Natixis, Crédit Agricole), three English (Barclays, HSBC, Royal Bank of Scotland), two German (Commerzbank and Deutsche Bank), one Swiss (UBS), one Canadian (Scotiabank), one Japanese (Nomura), and one Spanish (Santander) shared the cake.

The best. I use the imperfect tense because, while it was selective and profitable to be part of this club, 2020 was an *annus horribilis* for the sector. A tipping point when several banks decided to leave the club. Crédit Agricole and Santander abandoned ship. Others may follow. Lack of profitability was invoked...

Central banks, including the ECB, are prohibited from intervening directly in the markets. In practice, since the 2008 crisis, they have been making and holding prices. Without them, the markets would collapse. As a result, zero interest rates are becoming the norm.

I feel like I am ruining my story that started well, but I know roughly where I want to go... to China and Russia...

Everything thus appears locked on the financial planet but on the dark side of things. Far from the real world. Never in the light of the economy. States now have money for free. For example, Italy and Spain will receive, due to the crisis generated by the COVID pandemic, 108 billion for the former and 97 for the latter. Each will be able (among other things) to reimburse the endemic corruption in its economy, pay the bills of Cosa Nostra, and the stupidities of Juan Carlos... I know, I am being petty and unfair. And France? With its 40 billion, it will pay (in part) the truckloads of public money spent at Areva for (among other things) Uramin...

All this can happen because the system is locked and boosted by the central banks and by the markets, which are always inclined to make money without too much risk or effort. If the financial system were not so locked and did not operate in a closed circuit, this free money, the currency, the balance sheets of the central banks, and all the markets would fall into ruin. Like in *Star Wars* when Darth Vader plays with a lightsaber. Lockdown is the *sine qua non* of today's financial markets.

In the past, it was more open, competitive, and therefore relatively regulated by reality. Not here.

However, the guarantor of this lockdown remains the savings of the population, that is to say, the work from which it is the fruit. It is the ultimate reassurance of the system. This is what BlackRock would like to capture. And what must be prevented at all costs.

A pernicious movement has been set in motion. When the mechanism of arbitration and bailout of states begins to work, the country feels better. It is exactly like a heroin shot. It is complicated to stop this influx of money... unless we authoritatively decree what must be financed: Renault, Air France, or start-ups, for example. And what should not be: unemployment of intermittent workers, hair salons, artisan carpenters... Here, we see that choices become political... and that storytelling has its place... putting us to sleep, making us accept decisions that have no real basis, which lead to social and climatic catastrophes...

And in the end, what? And if we follow this financial logic to the end, where does it lead? No one, basically, works or pays themselves. That is the final outcome. The system is becoming more and more oligarchic. It is a very objective reality.

And for the people? Let's be brief and concise: the State decrees "Peace, games, and shut up!" Or a variation: "Police, football, and BFM". Well, a virus has grafted itself onto the story that complicates the equation. We can easily add a mask and a pandemic to the list.

A significant fraction of the people at the controls of this drifting system are convinced that they are democrats, acting for the common good, or doing the best they can, given the situation. That is the prevailing discourse. But they do not see that they are acting within the framework of an increasingly totalitarian system. What the European Commissioners, the Ministers and Deputy Ministers of the Economy or the Budget, or the President of the ECB say or think ultimately has little importance. The system has taken control, and they have become spectators with little room for maneuver, puppets in a play that is being acted out elsewhere.

Not being a conspiracy theorist, I am unable to say where and who is pulling these strings. I just know that there must be dominants, dominated, and intermediary bodies that are complicit with the dominants for the show to go on. There are no specific places or assemblies where decisions are made at a given moment. The play is acted out slowly, on many stages. A few countervailing powers exist.

But let's get back to this free money poured out by the central banks. We must think about its destination. Logically, it will end up invested in controlled and controllable assets, markets where high-frequency trading allows losses and evasions to be more or less controlled (BlackRock, Vanguard, etc.). Or in real estate, where prices are stable, or even rising.

Huge financial bubbles are occurring and will continue over time. With the consequences: ever more pressure on companies by the markets (we must deliver returns to shareholders), overpriced real estate, and pressurized employees. Layoff plans. Work for HR managers and slum landlords.

The outcome is easy to imagine: the discreet, exponential, and massive impoverishment of an entire country. Who wins? Banking intermediaries and those with capital. They will benefit first from credits: "We only lend to the rich", the tune is well-known.

Who loses? Everyone else. The entire population of a country. Let's say 90% compared to 10% in France. And again, I'm being generous with this statistic.

I digress a little, but it is to come back better...

China and Russia have other perspectives: their currencies are increasingly strong, they are storing gold, catching up with us on this side. They have little debt compared to us. They seem to think and make it known that the game will come to an end, that the key to unlocking the system could be the fall of the dollar. It would take with it the fragile currencies, supported by their central banks riddled with debt and assets bought on the markets at any price. Not sure that the euro will resist.

BlackRock has studied this scenario and is investing massively in Asia. The firm has just created a joint venture with a Chinese fund – this is a first – which opens up significant prospects for it and allows it to escape the restrictions of the Trump administration. For the Chinese, this is a nice snub that the current tenant of the White House must moderately appreciate.

The United States is managed like a hedge fund. The overall debt has far exceeded GDP, with a ratio of 1 to 3, which was exceeded since COVID. Sixty to one hundred million people are unemployed or dependent on food stamps. Life expectancy is declining, and nearly 1% of the American population is in prison. On the other hand, about 15% of the population lives well. In a country like the USA, private debt is essential. 50% of Americans have $1,000 in their accounts and no savings. Without revolving credit, the country cannot function, and Americans can neither live nor consume. For student loans alone, nearly 50 million Americans are still stuck in this system. And we are talking about 150 million people in debt. The figure is only increasing.

This is crazy. The USA is increasingly resembling the *Battleship Potemkin*. The balance has become very unstable.

Europe is lost, searching for itself, and dividing itself. China, Russia, and India are pushing. The confrontations that the United States is waging against China and its technologies have the appearance of desperate guerrilla warfare. Donald Trump's threats against the Chinese telecom giant Huawei are pathetic in this regard.

This subjugation of central banks to financial markets, systemic banks, and asset managers weighs on our present but above all obscures the future. Developments are too slow and are measured in generations. The risk of finding ourselves stuck is becoming conceivable. If we let it happen, we could end up with this generation (mine, let's say the baby boomers) penniless and annihilated. Several generations will have to live in this quagmire, with exceptional social damage that is already emerging at the start of the 2020 school year.

The Banque de France is playing with our future. We are trapped. In 1940, it protected gold and the country ten years in advance. This is no longer the case. Beyond the corruption cases, despite the credits granted to companies and the aid from Pôle emploi, the State appears sluggish. It is becoming both titanic and powerless, in a decline that is now visible. The visits of BlackRockers or other American pension funds that parade at the Élysée during more or less official meetings – especially the first one where we saw its president – are reminiscent of those made by the IMF in Argentina a few years ago... and here we are.

So what? I am going to say something crazy. Perhaps it would be wise to slowly and discreetly leave the euro. I see this as an extreme response, yet the euro has failed. It was designed to face globalization. It had to be a showcase for the German economy and, at the same time, a powerful monetary instrument for Europe in competition with the dollar. It has failed miserably. Neither the Central Bank nor the euro can find solutions. It is a major failure. We can easily measure it with the ECB's balance sheet, which went from 2 to 6,000 billion euros between 2008 and 2020. This fact alone is appalling. And if we take on a few billion more (600 for France for example), we will reach sums that are totally out of step with economic reality.

China will become the master of the world in 2030. Russia is advancing its pawns, and I do not believe that Europe will get out of it... unless the Germans say "Stop, let's go back to the Deutsche Mark", the French remember the saying "We want our life back", and finally, we have more radical solutions to change the present and the future.

Chapter 28

The real central bank should be the people. They are the ones who work, produce value, and generate money to store, spend, or invest, allowing us to reformulate our exchanges and our deep state into currency and debt. A central bank should be a service to its country and its citizens, not an out-of-control hydra that relies on BlackRock to supposedly save a nation's economy, while these all-powerful funds only wring it dry.

Central banks cannot collapse, especially today when they are heavily intertwined. They can create money as needed. This monetary inflation only makes sense if the economy works and produces value, growth, and employment. Otherwise, why work? Money is free... Free money kills the economy and creates huge real estate and financial market bubbles.

I'm off. I'm continuing. The quality of a currency lies in the strength and harmony of its economy. And right now, we are in the bright red, just before the gray and then the deep black. Unemployment is rising and almost everywhere reaches 20% of the active population, if we remove training, bogus internships, and erroneous statistics...

Before the COVID crisis, we had $75,000 billion of global GDP (the net cash available to pay for everything, invest, store) for $225,000 billion of global debts. The ratio of global debt to GDP was 3:1, meaning there were three times more debts than money coming in. (Here, we count the debts of individuals and companies in addition to public debts.) We find this ratio in many countries. Since COVID, the gap has widened further. In France, our global debt is approximately 2.5 times greater than our GDP. If we only consider public debts, the ratio is about 1.2 (public debts represent 120% of GDP). These data are estimates and describe a trend in a world exploring unknown territories and areas of debt never seen before. We are clearly living beyond our means, which would not be serious if the wheel could turn forever.

Are you still there?

In 1996, I happened to come across Viviane Forrester in debates or on TV sets. She had just written *L'Horreur économique* (Fayard), while I was releasing my first essay. My book explained my break with journalism at Libération and my vision of a corrupt France, under the influence of multinationals. Hers was a cry, initially the cry of a mother who had seen her son commit suicide and wanted to warn the world to beware of the liberal horror that was coming. We made a good duo. She was a bourgeois, a literary woman. I was a young journalist who resigned. She left this world in 2013. I am still here. She had found the right words, and her book would be successful in about twenty countries. The economic horror was everywhere: in the West, in Germany, in the USA, in Japan, in Italy, in Spain. I came across Viviane's book again in my library.

Here is what its back cover says: "We live in a masterful deception, a vanished world that artificial policies claim to perpetuate. Our concepts of work and therefore of unemployment, around which politics is played (or claims to be played), no longer have any substance: millions of lives are ravaged, destinies are destroyed by this anachronism. The general imposture continues to impose the systems of an outdated society so that a new form of civilization that is already emerging goes unnoticed, where only a very small percentage of the earth's population will find functions. The extinction of work passes for a simple eclipse while, for the first time in history, all human beings are less and less necessary to the small number who shape the economy and hold power. We discover that beyond the exploitation of men, there was worse, and that, faced with the fact of no longer even being exploitable, the crowd of men considered superfluous can tremble, and each man in this crowd. From exploitation to exclusion, from exclusion to elimination...?"

Twenty-four years have passed. And the answer to the distressing question posed by Viviane Forrester is yes. We have moved on to elimination. Social and physical killing. All human beings are, obviously, less and less necessary to the small number of human beings who shape the economy and hold power: the armies, the police, the banking system, the borders, the media.

When you think about it, the world functions like a big LBO. Sick credits. The wealthiest will always win, and the gap will widen and widen, without us being able to really react or stop the runaway trend.

The next financial crisis will probably cause the system to crack and the stock markets to plummet. In Davos this year, the tycoons who govern us have planned a way out if the worst-case scenario comes true. They called it the "great reset." At first, I thought it was a joke, but no. Find out. It's a reset of the (banking) counters, imagined by the thinkers at Davos...

To zero for us. Not really for them.

We can clearly see, reading these articles, including in the financial press, that the system's resistance to a major crisis would be almost zero. Everything can collapse quickly. The subprime crisis made it possible to measure the fragility of the system. What happened in 2008 could happen again, tenfold.

In 2008, states lent money to banks, but were not served in return. No bank has been nationalized in France, for example, where Nicolas Sarkozy still gave up €360 billion to save the banking system.

Today, debts have increased in each country, including Germany.

In this context, BlackRock has continued to capture savings massively. The BlackRockers are de facto, through this mass, in the wake of the central banks and key powers.

It is difficult to predict the future. Just object that the management is bad, the system is rotten, with enormous fragility factors.

BlackRock is one of them.

Today, few people—including at the top of the State—are aware of the fragilities of the system.

Systemic political reforms would be needed to get out of it.

We can clearly see here that three worlds are clashing: that of the nationalists who want a withdrawal into the countries by locking up the borders and throwing emigrants into the sea or into camps; that of the liberals who swear only by growth and the market; and that of the ecologists and the degrowth movement. I am not talking about the radical or soft left, nor the right, nor capitalism or anti-capitalism. These debates bore me and have become sterile.

During the lockdown, I remember the statements of the Minister of the Economy, Bruno Le Maire, who assured that companies linked to tax havens would no longer be helped by the State and that he would monitor and regulate (or even prohibit) dividend payments in times of crisis and scarcity. Nothing was undertaken or achieved. These promises were not worth a penny. AXA paid €3.6 billion to its shareholders. BNP, €3.9 billion, and Total, €1.8 billion. During the lockdown, the people suffered, but business continued, and insurance companies, banks, and oil groups distributed royal dividends to their shareholders, as if COVID were a joke. And us, collateral damage.

These companies, these multinationals, their shareholders, pension funds, investment banks, and BlackRock will never give up their jackpot. They are our adversaries, our enemies. It will be them and their cronies against us.

An op-ed published at the end of April 2020, which went relatively unnoticed, did indeed raise the question of these fractures: "Let's free society to emerge from the crisis," was the headline of the liberal right-wing newspaper owned by Arnaud Lagardère and now Bernard Arnault. It was signed by around sixty academics, economists, lobbyists, and second-rate figures such as Gérard Longuet, Dominique Reynié, and Virginie Calmels. All noted that the State had failed in managing the epidemic and called for fewer taxes, less taxation, a return to growth, and free markets. "There is no healthy democracy without a free market…," they droned on. I was interested in this op-ed because it contained all the clichés regularly heard on television sets. Its purpose was not to be read by a large number of people but to lay down milestones for later. It was labeled by the Republic on the Move and the liberal right.

It explained to us that they would be the globalizers, the supporters of even more unbridled liberalism, the manufacturers of a world after, worse than the one before. The opposite of us, who want to slow down, rethink growth, and the balance of political power.

A few weeks before, the philosopher and sociologist Bruno Latour, on the AOC site, had predicted this confrontation and also laid down markers: "Unfortunately, this sudden pause in the globalized production system is not only seen as a great opportunity by environmentalists to advance their landing program. The globalizers, those who since the middle of the 20th century have invented the idea of escaping planetary constraints, also see it as a great chance to break even more radically with what remains of obstacles to their escape from the world. The opportunity is too good for them to get rid of the rest of the welfare state, the safety net for the poorest, what remains of anti-pollution regulations, and, more cynically, to get rid of all these excess people who clutter the planet."

This question and this confrontation are being asked everywhere. The pandemic has shown us that everything can be stopped and rethought. Even if, since the end of the lockdown, the all-powerful propaganda machine has started up again. The situation is getting tense. If in France, Emmanuel Macron poses as the unifier of this huge broken world, he will not be able to repair it. He will be forced to manage a crisis that will not end with him.

Chapter 29

I am not a financial journalist. I try to sense the hidden intentions behind the mechanics and sequences presented to us. I delve into the mysteries. The storytelling that portrays the USA as our unwavering ally or suggests that the Stock Exchange drives the economy does not suit me. Nor does the narrative that paints Larry as a wise man, a generous individual, or a Benedictine. Similarly, I do not see Burry or Bogle as either young or old fools. I do not hold an ideological or catastrophic view of people or events. But I know that Larry is a shark. His driving force is his greed.

For a long time, I had the title "Larry the Embrouille" for this project. It suited the character and had an Audiard-like quality that I liked. A friend told me: "You know, before being considered a genius on Wall Street and saving the banks after the subprime crisis, he still bought tens of thousands of shares in Lehman Brothers three months before its collapse. Everyone has forgotten that. As a snitch, we can do better. This guy has a knack for confusing us. He is a true genius at trickery..."

Embrouille (feminine noun): Disorder aimed at confusing or deceiving; an abuse of elements of confusion. A bag of tangles (a bag of knots). To entangle, to wrap up, to smoke.

Larry is the boss, the thinker, and the totem man of BlackRock throughout the world. And wherever the multinational goes, BlackRock is nothing but a nest of tangles. Where BlackRock goes, the light dies. This would be my slogan if I had to launch a campaign.

I could give you a thousand examples, but I don't want to overload your neurons. Mine are overheating. If you've followed me this far, without tiring yourself out too much, I've already won.

It's January 2012. Wall Street brokers have anonymously complained to New York police officers about pressure and blackmail being exerted on them by

BlackRock. The cops wouldn't have moved if the alerted attorney general, who is particularly sensitive to these issues, hadn't motivated them. BlackRock executives were accused of forcing brokers and financial analysts in New York State to give them confidential information about their work and the situation of their clients. The BlackRockers denied the accusations. The attorney general ended up suing BlackRock for insider trading. An accusation that immediately alarmed Larry. He put his best lawyers on the case.

The problem is the prosecutor. His name is Eric Schneiderman. He is young and has a reputation for being a tough guy. He is the magistrate who wants to save Gotham City in Batman. He accuses the firm not only of recording confidential information to which it has access as a shareholder but, above all, of "using its dominant position to force Wall Street brokers and analysts to respond to very detailed investigations into their activities." The investigation showed that BlackRock had set up an ingenious system of rewards for those who collaborated and of reprimands for those who refused to comply. All this information, sometimes confidential, fed into the matrix of Aladdin.

I insist on this story because it is little known in Europe and has not caused much stir across the Atlantic. There are a few scattered articles on the websites of the New York Times, Bloomberg, or Politico. BlackRock's communicators and lawyers are known for confusing the press. In many ways, they remind me of those at Clearstream.

On September 24, 2013, Eric Schneiderman was invited to a conference organized by the Bloomberg press agency. He was then in the middle of an investigation into BlackRock's insider trading. He did not mention Larry's name, but everyone thought of him when the magistrate mentioned those who pervert the markets and display great greed. This first speech and the indictment that followed shattered the propaganda of Wall Street's rising star, Larry Fink, and his firm, the largest asset manager in the world—protector of retirees and small savers.

Today, I think we need to rethink some of our habits because we're seeing something far more insidious than traditional insider trading. Quiet but powerful groups are able to use public information combined with high-frequency trading in ways that distort our markets far more than Albert Wiggin, Ivan Boesky, or Gordon Gekko could ever have imagined. This combination of high-frequency trading with access to nonpublic information, illegally obtained in advance, is what we call "insider trading 2.0" in my office. This is the first time the term has been used, and the comparison to the BlackRock boss is apt. Albert Wiggin was a greedy banker who got rich off the backs of the poor during the Great Depression. Ivan Boesky, a stock trader who fell in 1986, is a champion insider who got rich by obtaining information from his inner circle. After an SEC investigation and confessions, he admitted his wrongdoings and served three and a half years in prison. He paid a $100 million fine without flinching to avoid further punishment. Boesky inspired the character of Gordon Gekko, the cynical and lawless Wall Street trader, in Oliver Stone's blockbuster film. Boesky is known for a cult tirade in which he claims his greed for profit as a way of life: "I think greed is healthy. You can be greedy and feel good about yourself."

Any comments, Larry?

And the prosecutor, inspired that day, continued along the same lines: In the 1960s, people held their stocks for an average of five years, which allowed them to create value. Now, the average holding period is estimated to be less than five days. In a minority of cases, some experts estimate it is less than a minute. No one buys stocks because of their value anymore. No one invests in stocks for a few hours or a few days to start a business or develop a product. It is simply incompatible with the basic ideas of our markets. It is becoming necessary to tackle this problem if we want to restore public confidence.

Before concluding:

When I was a child, everyone wanted to play the stock market. The symbols of wealth were owning your house and a portfolio of stocks. Average, normal Americans thought that they and their brokers, if they were prudent, had the opportunity to buy low and sell high like the big players on Wall Street did. But the new market manipulators—the ones doing something unimaginable a decade ago—are calling the savings of these average Americans "dumb money." And, ladies and gentlemen, many of us here may very well be among those owners of "dumb money." Because unless you have access to a supercomputer that can flip tens of thousands of stocks in milliseconds and access market information a little ahead of everyone else, you may be in "dumb money," even if you think you're an insider. When blinding speed is combined with rapid access to data, it gives people the power to extract value from the markets even before it reaches the rest of the Street. Four months later, after two years of investigation and heated debates, on January 8, 2014, the Attorney General of the State of New York and BlackRock reached an agreement under which BlackRock would agree to "end its program of surveys of Wall Street analysts". Eric Schneiderman signed the end of hostilities with Larry Fink and BlackRock. The firm was ordered to pay $400,000 in reimbursement of expenses. A tip that leaves a bitter taste for some observers or actors in the procedure... Schneiderman nevertheless took the time to denounce BlackRock's practices of "systematically aggregating" analysts' information, thus giving them an "unfair advantage in predicting future analyst opinions, in violation of the law". The investigation was thorough, but the prosecutor was unable to prove that strategic information had been delivered. BlackRock had been receiving secret reports from financial experts for five years, even though federal law prohibits brokerage firms from selectively disclosing information before it is released to eligible clients. The influx was far greater than the firm's lawyers argued in the lawsuit. The confidential information underpinned Aladdin's power and notoriety. BlackRock has neither admitted nor denied the attorney general's findings but has "agreed to remedial measures, including a permanent, worldwide halt to the investigative program and continued cooperation with ongoing related investigations."

Because the pressure on analysts and other wealth managers extended beyond New York to the world. In a lengthy statement, Eric Schneiderman announced that the settlement ends the practice of systematically questioning Wall Street analysts to obtain information about the companies they advise.

Before the settlement, BlackRock operated the largest investigative program in the world, soliciting responses from brokers who unwillingly revealed unpublished material in their reports. Analyst reports are considered information that has a significant impact on the market and investor decisions. The attorney general's office determined that the design, timing, and structure of the investigations allowed BlackRock to obtain information that was used to, as a BlackRock document put it, preempt future analyst revisions. The BlackRock investigation was based in part on information provided by confidential whistleblowers who came forward to express serious concerns and pressure. The attorney general's office obtained hundreds of thousands of pages of documented evidence related to BlackRock's analyst investigation program and gathered testimony from BlackRock employees and others.

The statement buries the proceedings in a brutal and "incomprehensible" manner, according to some investigators frustrated at not having pursued the investigation further: "They promised to arrest, so we let it go, like a judge releasing a fence because he promised to arrest, without even investigating the criminals for whom he was fencing," said one witness. In this case, it would have been interesting to know to whom BlackRock was selling its illegally collected information—probably to hedge funds or algorithmic trading funds...

In his biography or during interviews when he comes to Europe, Larry is never asked about these gray areas. He spends his life making people believe that he works for the good of retirees and small savers, while his goal remains to pick our pockets. He is a real pickpocket. A first-rate huckster. A champion of double-dealing. We listen to him, he smiles, he explains to us that we are has-beens with our public services and our thirty-five-hour week. He dies laughing when we talk about retiring at sixty or reducing working hours.

Macron pats him on the back. And it is us who are in pain.

I continue to charge the mule. But rest assured, it smells like a stable…

For example, Larry calls himself a Democrat, supported Hillary Clinton, and supports Joe Biden but does not criticize the Republicans. Worse, in December 2016, he proudly joined a business forum convened by Donald Trump to "provide strategic and political advice on economic issues."

Don't forget that several of his friends and sponsors in the business supported Trump's campaign and his policy of market deregulation.

Larry has made a lot of money for his clients, he makes a lot of money for himself, but he has also lost a lot. There is, of course, the story of the failed loans of First Boston ($100 million), but there are especially reckless purchases like Stuyvesant Town, a real estate complex of one hundred and ten buildings, acquired in 2006 for $5.4 billion in Manhattan. He made the Californian pension fund CalPERS lose $500 million, a big loser who will not hold it against him too much… Larry believed in it, as he believes in ETFs, but he had not anticipated any of the additional costs of the construction site. He is sometimes, despite Aladdin, very short-sighted.

So far, he has always gotten out of these troubles without a hitch. Larry is a cat. An acrobat. A primitive but sophisticated being. He is a crafty peasant who collects, as we have seen, in a bulimic way, what he calls "American folklore," popular art with a Wild West style. Do you remember Sheila's song? "I don't know if you are like me But every time it makes me happy To listen to an old tune of American folklore being played on a crincrin Immediately I see myself already in the depths of Arizona Wearing a big hat and strumming on an old banjo Woh Ring ding ding." I am sure Larry would love these old-fashioned lyrics, easy to remember and hum, extolling the joy of living in America. Sheila's 45 rpm record may be sitting in her museum between a signed Brian Wilson record and a pipe that belonged to Buffalo Bill. Larry is a simple guy. A collector. He endlessly amasses piles of worthless objects. His North Salem weather vanes. We are far from the Rembrandt paintings of Wall Street billionaire Thomas Kaplan or the flashy, tax-free contemporary art of Bernard Arnault. All this ostentatious crap is too expensive, too complicated. Larry claims this typical taste of the "farmer," like a barn where mountains of odds and ends accumulate, just in case, you never know. When he was a student, he drank beers and participated in secret society gatherings that today bring together the biggest bankers on the planet. Some, even in the so-called serious press, see them as occult governments. Take a look at Kappa Neta Phi, the fraternity where Larry is prominently featured between Michael Bloomberg, the former mayor of NYC, and Robert Rubin, the former vice president of Goldman Sachs and former Secretary of the Treasury. It looks more like a gathering of old students nostalgic for a white, macho America. Their insignia consists of a beer mug, a champagne glass, a hand with a pointing finger, and five stars. Their Latin motto, Dum vivamus edimus et biberimus, means "While we live, we eat and drink." True.

Larry started his career with a big mortgage bust at First Boston. Then he rode the subprime scandal to bounce back to Wall Street, where his reputation as a winner was highlighted in a very long profile published by Vanity Fair. Sixteen pages in Vanity. The consecration. Although when he read it, Larry coughed. And so did we. The highlight of the article is this short passage that really annoyed Larry, who makes such an effort to police his speech: "People liked him, but he was also seen as arrogant and rude, like 'a guy who always wanted more than he got,'" says a former partner at First Boston. He was drooling, his nose pressed against the window. You could feel his intense ambition. He made huge bets on the markets, happy to constantly push the limits," adds the Vanity journalist. He is also remembered as a big swinging dick, a BSD, a phrase immortalized by Michael Lewis in his book *Liar's Poker*. He was trying to describe the most arrogant and aggressive of Wall Street bond traders. Years later, Fink reacted bitterly to this description, citing the snobbery of Wall Street investment bankers, who looked down on Jewish or Italian traders (like him) and who were allowed to succeed in the mortgage bond business only "because no one else would have them." The article also refers to BlackRock as "a shadow government," referring to the mountain of government contracts awarded to it. The term "shadow government" used in the Vanity Fair article is very relevant.

Many observers consider BlackRock's dominance to be a major problem. The company manages nearly $10 trillion in assets, a figure that dwarfs the budgets of most countries. In other words, BlackRock's share of the world's economy is larger than most nations' economies. The entity is the largest shareholder in almost every major company. It is hard to imagine the full implications of such power. The company holds vast amounts of data, has significant influence over global markets, and, by extension, over world politics.

A good friend of Larry's recently observed: "I was a close friend of Larry Fink. He was not a charmer but a man of his time who was close to nothing. A big opportunist who started his career in real estate, a person who really wanted to show he could sell anything. He worked at a high level with First Boston, then he joined BlackRock, a company that became a powerful tool of finance that no one ever suspected would grow so much. A very astute man, endowed with a considerable intelligence that was quite unusual at the time. He is a man who saw a great deal of financial opportunity when others, including many talented people, could not see it." Larry became known as a master of financial engineering. To him, finance is a game. He runs BlackRock like a machine. He sees everything through the prism of numbers. For him, the only reality is financial performance.

Epilogue

While searching the Internet to find BlackRock's investments in French vineyards, I discovered "black rot" or black rot. This is a vine disease caused by a fungus native to North America. It has invaded European vineyards and is highly contaminating, invasive and complex to treat. It dries out and "mummifies" the grapes. Its attack is almost undetectable because the poisoning is root-borne and comes from the soil. When the fruit is attacked, it is too late to save the vines. It is generally necessary to destroy the contaminated plots, treat them with products that kill Black Rot and replant. This disease is described as explosive and very damaging to vineyards, because rain accelerates its spread.

The analogy is too good not to be mentioned. We have a lot to learn from nature...

Don't miss out!

Visit the website below and you can sign up to receive emails whenever Edward Branson publishes a new book. There's no charge and no obligation.

https://books2read.com/r/B-A-KPLMC-EMSAF

BOOKS 2 READ

Connecting independent readers to independent writers.